Decentralization and Development
The Korean Experience

Decentralization and Development-The Korean Experience

Printed in Seoul, Republic of Korea

Seoul National University Press
599 Gwanak-ro, Gwanak-gu, Seoul 151–742, Republic of Korea

E-mail: snubook@snu.ac.kr
Home-page: http://www.snupress.com
Tel: 82-2-880-5252
Fax: 82-2-889-0785

First Printing: Dec. 20, 2010
ISBN: 978-89-521-1103-6 93300

Decentralization and Development

The Korean Experience

Edited by

Tobin Im

Seoul National University Press

Dedication

In Commemoration of Korean Association of Local Government Studies' 20th Anniversary

List of Contributers

Tobin Im is Chair of Seoul National University's Graduate School of Public Administration. Professor Im was awarded a Ph.D. in Organizational Sociology from l'Institute d'Etudes Politiques de Paris, and has published numerous articles in world class academic journals such as Public Administration Review. In addition to articles he has also published many books in Korea, France, Holland, Russia and India. His research and teaching areas of interest include organizational theory, performance management, and comparative administration. In an effort to create an Asian model of public administration, his current research deals with how to apply the 'time' concept to various realms of public affairs. E-mail: tobin@snu.ac.kr

Soon Eun Kim is a professor in the Department of Public Administration at Dong-eui University, Korea. His teaching and research focus is on local government, urban politics, local finance, intergovernmental relations, and comparative political systems. E-mail: sekim@deu.ac.kr

Yunho Kang is a professor in the Department of Maritime Administration at Korea Maritime University, Korea. His teaching and research focus is on local government, maritime administration and financial management. E-mail: yhkang@hhu.ac.kr

Seung Rak Choi is a professor in the Department of managment at Dongyang Technical College, Korea. His research focus is on Leisure & Entertainment industry policy. E-mail: haihaba@chol.com

Ki-Shik Lee is a professor in the Department of Public Administration at Hanzhong University, Korea. His teaching and research focus is on information system management, cyber citizen participation and e-government. E-mail: elee@korea.com

Minah Kang is a member of the Department of Public Administration at Ewha Women's University, Korea. Her teaching and research focus is on health care policy, welfare policy and research methods. E-mail: minahkang@ewha.ac.kr

Sang-Cheoul Lee is a professor in the Department of Public Administration at Pusan National University, Korea. His research interests focus on bureaucratic (organizational) reform and public enterprise (quasi-government). E-mail: sclee7923@pusan.ac.kr

Sung-Bae Kim is a professor in the Department of Public Administration at Soongsil University, Korea. His teaching and research focus is on local public administration, urban public administration and land policy. E-mail: graal@ssu.ac.kr

Kwang Ju Kim is a professor in the Department of Public Administration at Kyungil University, Korea. His teaching and research focus is on intergovernmental relations, administrative behavior, and public management. E-mail: kjkim@kiu.ac.kr

Dool-sun Kim is a BK21 Post-Doc researcher in the Department of Public Administration at Ewha Women's University, Korea. E-mail: kimdully@hanmail.net

Wonhyuk Cho is a Ph.D. candidate of Seoul National University's Graduate School of Public Administration. E-mail: wonhyukcho@gmail.com

Gregory Porumbescu is a Ph.D. candidate in the Graduate School of Public Administration at Seoul National University and full time lecturer in the Department of Public Administration at Kyonggi University, Korea. E-mail: gporumbescu@hotmail.com

CONTENTS

Part III Citizen Participation

Part IV Administrative Efficiency

Part V Conclusion

Preface

The term "local autonomy" or "decentralization" had not been popular in Korea in the past assuming that the local autonomous system might have had a negative influence on national economic development, in particular since 1961, when local self-governments ceased to exist anymore. The central government only had made and implemented policies. People believed that the centralized system, like the military, was an efficient tool to achieve fast development.

The Korean Association of Local Autonomy Studies (KALAS) was established in 1988 when there were no local governments. As a result of devoted efforts made by senior scholars, including professor Yung Hee Nho, professor An Je Kim, professor Se Uk Jung, professor Chang Ho Choi, professor Sang Cheol Cho, and others, KALAS has now become a major association in Korea which includes numerous academia and practitioners. KALA has published the principal journal in the field of decentralization, Korean Association of Local Autonomy Studies since December 1998.

KALAS has always been the central organization for discussing issues related to decentralization reform and the debates and the papers published in KALAS Journal consequently have tremendously influenced government decision makers. It is hard to disassociate KALAS activities from the Korean history of decentralization. Korea has experienced unique and valuable decentralization reforms. This book aims to commemorate KALAS 20th anniversary in December 2008.

In fact KALAS planned several special events for its 20th anniversary, including a special seminar in which deeper analyses of the Korean local autonomy were to be carried out, and the publication of a book intended to introduce the Korean local autonomy to foreign readers in English.

Professor Tobin Im, editor-in-chief of the Journal of the Korean Association of Local Government Studies, has played a major role in planning and editing papers regarding Korean local autonomy. Additionally Professor Young, a leading public administration theorist in United States of America had also given valuable comments to the authors after reading the first drafts of the manuscripts.

Hopefully, this edited book will make a contribution to understanding Korean local autonomy for English speaking readers.

Soon Eun Kim
President of
Korean Association of Local Government Studies, 2008

Part I

Introduction

Chapter 1 |

Introduction

TOBIN IM

Why Decentralization?

South Korea, over the course of the past fifty years, has become one of the newly developed countries and is now far removed from the underdeveloped country she once was. She was one of the poorest countries in the world during the 1950's following the harsh Japanese colonization period which lasted from 1920 to 1945. This period of colonization was then followed by the Korean War (1950–1953) which led to more severe and widespread poverty thus depriving many of even the most basic goods and often times resulting in starvation. Consequently the Gross National Income for the year of (GNI) 1953 was 67 USD. However, the South Korea of today has exhibited phenomenal growth, a fact which can be best exemplified by a GNI of 9,358 USD for the year of 1999 and a growth rate of nearly 200 percent over the past 60 years.

Surprised by the dizzying pace of growth, many westerners refer to her as, in addition to Hong Kong, Taiwan, and Singapore, an Asian Dragon or Tiger. However when compared with the other Asian Tigers, South Korea should be considered a special case because its size is much larger than the other three countries. South Korea's territory is 1 million 32km^3 and its population nearly 48,600,000 as of 2008, thus making it much larger than any of the other Asian Tigers and rendering it incomparable with the other three countries. Furthermore, because the economy which accompanied the large population and geographic area was also much larger than the other four Asian Tiger's, the process of developing her government was also much more complex.

It is regrettable that most explanations related to the successful economic growth of Korea just focus on economic factors. The Economy is not everything for a country, especially when the internal politics become more complex as the people's political conscience matures. In a sense, political development is the most important factor when it comes to durable economic development for a developing country like Korea because without it economic development would cease. We have ample examples of countries who suffer from democratization 'fever' across the world. Although they tried to introduce western styled democracy, their absolute poverty does not allow them to see the true effect of democratic reforms; military coups, corruption, high infant mortality, environmental destruction, etc. all detract from their ability to successfully launch, implement and realize the potential of such reforms.

This book challenges the fundamental question about the relationship between development and democratization. More specifically democratization here means decentralization. What effects have the decentralization reforms had on a country like South Korea? In a sense, the Korean case serves as a testing ground for many countries who suffer from the chronic problems mentioned above.

However discussing the relationship between the decentralization reforms and development is not as simple as one might think. The first hurdle to overcome here is how to define or confine the concept of development in order to advance this argument. Obviously development means economic growth which improves people's lives. Nevertheless, improving the material aspects of people's lives is not all that is required for the development of a country. Political development mainly means to empower the ordinary people by transferring centralized political power from a dictator or an elite group to the people. In addition, all nations, and especially developing ones, need to have an efficient government as a policy tool, because despite the importance of the market, governments play a locomotive role in almost all aspects of the society. Considering these three dimensions of development, one can raise three related questions as follows;

- What economic effects have Korean local governments had after the decentralization reforms?
- To what extent has citizen participation been taken and how?
- Do decentralization reforms increase administrative efficiency of local governments?

This book consists of three parts, in addition to the Introduction, with each part attempting to answer these three questions. The chapter authors explain, argue and discuss their specific issue either theoretically, empirically or both.

To provide readers with some background information for better understanding, chapter 2 analyzes historical developments and describes the major characteristics of intergovernmental relations in Korea since 1948. Korea has had its own unique history of decentralization, and what can be considered most unique is the rapid transition of her political system from a centralized on to a decentralized one. In the course of decentralization there have been a lot of power politics and to a large extent the successful results of the decentralization reforms were only possible as a result of a bloody struggle for the democratization of the country.

However the recent decentralization is not enough to understand the Korean history of decentralization. Developments of intergovernmental relations in Korea have fluctuated since 1948 in light of certain circumstances and can be divided into four different periods (Kim, 2008) although the precise divisions of the periods are slightly different among political scientists (Choi et al., 2004). The first period is between 1948 and 1960 while the second period spans from 1961 to 1979. The third period extends from 1980 to 1990 while the fourth period began in 1991 and continues until present.

The year of 1948 was historically significant because the political identity of Korea, that is the Republic of Korea, was established on the basis of a modern constitution in which articles related to local autonomy were inserted for the first time in Korean history. The year of 1960 was a turning point when the dictatorship of the Rhee Administration collapsed due to the Student Revolutions on April 19, 1960. The Second Republic which followed the Student Revolutions tried to develop a democratic regime in which intergovernmental relations between the central government and local governments were possible.

The years between 1980 and 1990 was a period when local autonomy, which was abolished by the Military Coup of May 16th 1961, became a political issue and regarded as a tool for improving Korean democracy.

Eventually, Korean local autonomy was resumed in 1991 and has since increased the role of intergovernmental relations in Korea and has lead to big differences. In particular, the Roh Moo Hyun Administration which started in 2003 had tried to devolve considerable powers to local governments.

Decentralization and Economic Growth

The relationship between decentralization reform and economic growth is not evident as the previous studies do not provide consistent conclusions about this relationship (Martinez-Vazquez and McNab, 2003). Splitting decision making power into many smaller units by instituting local governments might increase economic growth of the country by way of regional development, however decentralization can also result in inefficiency in terms of time and resource management because too many veto points arise thereby negatively affecting the consensus building process when compared with a centralized government imposing policies upon local entities. These two opposing hypotheses both offer strong supporting arguments.

Chapter 3 tackles this debatable issue by placing an emphasis on changes which have occurred over time in the sample countries, and focuses on the Korean case. Korea has experienced rapid economic growth under a strongly centralized state tradition and consequently it is interesting to see how Korea's decentralization reforms during the 1990's affected its economic growth. Even though decentralization is considered as a good direction of reform, the question of right timing remains in the Korean case.

Considering the availability of valid data, this study includes only 34 developing countries covering annual observations from 1970 to 2007. As independent variables, the degree of decentralization is measured by fiscal decentralization and political decentralization. Economic growth as a dependent variable is measured by the annual growth rate of the country concerned. The results based on time a series model reveal that decentralization can increase the administrative capacity of a country from a certain period. If decentralization reforms are introduced earlier than this time period, it will make the decision-making system inefficient by inundating the system with many peripheral issues and reducing its ability to focus on the critical issues for the development of the country.

Introducing decentralization reform is expected to bring about a fundamental shift in paradigm. In the centralized era, the Korean governments had mobilized all national resources to concentrate on economic development. This 'economy first' strategy left issues of social inequality as side effects. Elected local officials are supposed to focus on local realities rather than national economic indicators.

Officials from the central government tend to understand and assess public affairs through summative statistics and therefore sacrifice the ability to see a more detailed reality. On the other hand the mayors and councilmen look closely at the quality of life their electoral constituencies possess. At this juncture it is legitimate to raise the question of whether decentralization has made local governments more oriented toward social welfare.

Chapter 4 attempts to test this policy orientation hypothesis. After having categorized local policy orientation into four types; 1) development-oriented, 2) welfare-oriented, 3) both (development and welfare)-oriented, 4) both-avoided, this chapter demonstrates policy orientation by using logistic regression modeling. The results of the statistical analysis failed to find a single and decisive conclusion about this research question, rather the types of policy orientation depend on each respective government's socioeconomic and political attributes.

Local governments compete with each other not only at the national level, but also at the international level. The theory of Tiebout(1956)'s foot democracy resulted in local officials focusing on economic growth of the region and boosting the economy by creating jobs. As a result they are now ready to do whatever it takes to bring growth to the local economy, no matter how small that growth might be. An example of this is Macao's successful gambling industry which inspired many countries across the world to consider opening casinos.

Korea, well known for its rigorous Confucius culture which emphasizes morality by dematerializing life, is not an exception in this regard. Chapter 5 investigates the true impact of development brought about by the opening of Kangwon Land Casino. Thus factors such as the population, the number of businesses and employees, road density, financial independence, and land prices will be assessed.

Seeing as the Kangwon Land Casino was built to promote the local development of the Jeongseon area in Gangwondo, an economically underdeveloped region, some people worried about the possibility of negative effects. However, overall many people embraced the idea of building casinos based on the belief that they can have a Midas touch on an area and lead to improved local growth. Consequently in East Asia, most cases of building casinos are not just viewed as a simple business but rather seen as a means of promoting an entire local economy. However, can the success of casinos really ensure local development? The success of a casino creates a lot of revenue and profit but, can the success of casinos result in the true advancement of an area or country? To answer this question we investigated whether the opening of Kangwon Land Casino has had a positive impact on the local development within the abandoned coalmine areas.

Perhaps, the development of the Kangwon Land Casino can be seen as having a certain degree of positive influence on the local development of Jeongseon County only, due to the fact that the casino is entirely located there. However there has been little to no effect in terms of local development in any other abandoned coalmine areas in the region. Although Kangwon Land Casino itself has enjoyed significant growth both in revenue and profit, the growth of the casino business appears to have had only a minimal impact on local development.

Citizen Participation and Decentralization

Citizen participation in local affairs is a critical factor in the process of decentralization, because the transition from a centralized system of goverenance to a decentralized one implies transferring decision making power from the central bureaucracy to the citizen. Along these lines we can therefore assume that allowing local citizens to decide issues relevant to them is the basic philosophy of decentralization. Participation is one of the relevant indicators used in measuring political development. There are two aspects of citizen participation; cyber participation and physical or traditional participation.

Especially, objects and space are sophisticated by the web 2.0 extension, UCC activation, and new trends to pursue participation and public ownership are being created because real-time collection and exchange of information is now possible at anytime and anywhere. This improvement of information communication technology has had a strong effect on the public sector as well as private sector.

In the case of Gangnam-gu, Seoul, Cyber Citizen Participation (CCP) has become very meaningful in making direct democracy possible through the internet, and demonstrating the importance and potential energy of citizen participation. There are many ways to use IT for enhancing direct participation.

People are so busy that it is hard for them to attend council meetings or to participate in the policy processes of their local governments. Citizens become selfish to the extent that they do not care as far as their interests are not concerned. Normally when assessing the costs of direct participation for the citizen, special attention needs to be paid to the incentive structure when designing a system of local governance. However, participation by internet costs almost nothing.

The benefits of cyber participation are enormous as it can improve the reliability and the efficiency of the local government's policy by building bridges between policy authenticity and transparency and additionally increase citizens' interest in local affairs' administration. CCP has brought about a change to new local self-governing and administrative paradigms and can be argued as having the intent of enhancing the diffusion of new information and methods of collecting opinions. In addition, internet has the potential to inform inhabitants of political measures and acts and also provides the people with a platform from which they can state their opinions (Brants, Huizenga and Meerten, 1996). People have experienced many spectacular effects thanks to the internet in areas such as electoral campaigns as well in demonstrations. These spectacular effects were essentially possible thanks to cyber debates. Thus a debating venue in the public sphere is constructed, and consequently it is expected that more reasonable policies with minimum errors are composed, executed, and evaluated. However special caution is needed in regards to the negative side effects of this new instrument of communication.

However, despite the fantastic effects the internet has had on political processes, direct participation by classic means of local democracy such as initiatives, calling, voting etc. are still the most important tools for decentralization. Theoretically it is interesting to see how local people begin to use their participation rights when they are afforded this power by decentralization reforms.

Chapter 7 investigates the role of citizen participation in local policy decision making based on the case of a water fluoridation program. This is an exciting case for understanding how people's behavior has changed since decentralization, because the water fluoridation is a scientifically debatable issue. Regarding an issue of scientific uncertainty, do the people act according to the scientific truth or their political considerations? Several interesting features stand out as follows.

First, since the introduction of local governance systems, the desire for participation of local citizen groups and residents in local health policy decision making was significantly increased and has consequently had an important impact on local democracy. At the same time, it made the local government and the local assembly more sensitive to pressures coming from citizen groups and the subsequent changes in the public opinion. Local governments especially appeared to be sensitive when responding to opposing opinions that were raised by citizen groups. Such tendencies were clearly shown in the case of the water fluoridation program, as we found that a number of programs were suspended even though there was no visible opposition activity in the pertinent area, instead opposition activities were primarily found in the neighborhood areas. There is a mutual learning process for the citizens as well as for the local officials who are newly elected in order to fully benefit from decentralization. Collective action theory will be a powerful tool of reasoning in this field (Olson, 1971).

Administrative Efficiency and Decentraization

The historical success of Korea's economic development is largely attributed to its strong and efficient government bureaucracy (Chibber, 2002). If Korean governmental bureaucracy, under a centralized system is among the most efficient when compared to other similar countries, a question of key interest would be whether the efficiency of the public sector has decreased since the introduction of decentralization reforms (Im, 2005). Increasing government's efficiency is the dominant preoccupation for the managers of the government machines, due to the fact that people become aware of wasted tax money.

Making government 'small' is among the most popular slogans used by candidates during election campaigns; however bureaucracy never stops growing (Parkinson, 1958). This is the reason why New Public Management has been the most influential theory in government reforms across the world since 1980's. New public management is often prescribed to reduce the government's size by looking to the private sector either by outsourcing or devolution. However, the validity of this imported philosophy of government reform in the Asian context is questioned by some scholars (Im, 2007).

The successful cases of implementing NPM reforms are revealed sometimes just as political rhetoric. However a closer look reveals that the reality of the government remains as before; instead of politicians affecting real change the merely pretend to have significantly changed the inertia of the bureaucracy. At this point we must begin to consider the fundamental question of, 'What is the true size of the government? '

Chapter 9 examines the proliferation of shadow organizations from the perspective of the quasi-autonomous governmental organization (quago), which is a ubiquitous feature of modern public governance. First, we need to raise questions in general regarding how the numbers of quagos have increased and what the main reasons are for their expansion.

One of the interesting questions is whether this expansion of the shadow organization is associated with decentralization reforms. What needs to be looked at is why the number of quagos increased after Korea implemented its system of local autonomy in 1995, when the central government's authority was delegated to the local governments through political and administrative decentralization.

If this phenomenon is not desirable, the next question to raise is how to enhance the socio-economic accountability behind the rapid growth of local quagos. For instance, one can think of monitoring quagos as a way of keeping optimal control but eventually recommendations focusing on under what conditions the local quagos perform best are required.

Controlling bureaucratic expansion is a necessary condition for increasing efficiency. A condition for this is how to satisfactorily deliver sufficient services to the citizen. This leads us to question the quality of government work which is largely determined by the quality of public services. In a centralized system, public services can be produced at a low cost thanks to economies of scale. However there are risks of waste in this system. In addition, the uniformity of services can satisfy citizen's needs which are diverse and dependent upon the places citizens live. This argument leads us to question the service delivery system.

Chapter 9 deals with the methods of public service delivery. Based on theoretical arguments and relevant cases, this chapter focuses on the relative efficacy between centralized governance and decentralized governance in the delivery of public service. The Centralized governance of public service delivery means (implies) that the field offices of central government are responsible for production of public services, whereas under decentralized governance, the central government delegates this function to local units of government. Empirically, cases such as road construction and maintenance show that the centralized system seems to be more efficient than decentralized governance in terms of making concerned agents work hard. It was also found that the provider of the national road service tends to make more relevant investments under centralized governance. This is a finding which somewhat supports the notion that centralization rather than the decentralization is more conducive to efficiency. However, the problems of corrupt politicians and bureaucrats appear to be higher under centralized governance than under decentralized.

Korea ranked first in a poll of countries regarding e-government (West, 2008). Information Technology (IT) Infrastructure is considered the most advanced in the world and Korean people use a lot this advanced technology. Information technology and the internet are miraculous tools for improving administrative efficiency if applied wisely. The internet geographical information system (GIS) opens a new way to expand geographic e-government.

With the help of the internet, this comprehensive GIS could have diverse impacts on the organization, behavior and quality of public services. It is in this context that chapter 10 examines the developmental process of GIS, the characteristics of GIS, and limitations of GIS applications on local government in Korea. Even though GIS applications to Korean local government are still in their infancy, it is very insightful to evaluate the Korean experience in order to learn about this new issue.

Like other policy areas, the central government had guided the construction of GIS in local governments. However there are weak connections between major GIS components such as planning and implementation and other areas. It is important to have a full exchange of information in order for such a program to have a synergetic effect on other IT programs which require large amounts of investment.

In the course of constructing GIS, local governments in Korea are facing technical limitations, organization behavioral and cultural limitations, legal and institutional limitations, database related limitations as well as others. Any one of these limitations could lead to the failure of GIS in local government. For successful geographic information and technology administration, this chapter tries to recommend alternative approaches such as cost efficient GIS, decentralized GIS and citizen-oriented GIS.

References

Brants, K., M., Huizenga and R., van Meerten. 1996. The Canals of Amsterdam: An Exercise in Local Electronic Democracy, *Media, Culture and Society* 18(2): 233–47.

Chibber, V. 2002. Bureaucratic Rationality and the Developmental State, *American Journal of Sociology* 107(4).

Choi, Y. and D., Wright. 2004. Intergovernmental Relation (IGR) in Korea and Japan: Phases, Patterns, and Progress toward Decentralization (Local Autonomy) in a Trans-pacific Context, *International Review of Public Administration* 9(1): 1–22.

Im, T. 2004. Action Theory for Local Organizations, Seoul: Pakyoung-sa.

_______. 2005. Comparative Public Administration, Seoul: Pakyoung-sa.

_______. 2007. Bureaucracy, Democracy, and Market Principle, *Korean Public Administration Review* 41(3): 41–65.

Kim, S. 2008. Intergovernmental Relations in Korea. In *Korean Association for Local Autonomy Studies* ed. Understanding of Korea Local Autonomy, Seoul: Parkyoungsa.

Martinez-Vazquez, J. and R.M., McNab. 2003. Fiscal Dece-ntralization and Economic Growth, *World Development* 31(9): 1597–616.

Olson, M. 1971. The Logic of Collective Action, Cambridge, MA: Harvard University Press.

Parkinson, T. 1958. Parkinson's Law: The Pursuit of Progress, London: John Murray.

Tiebout, C. 1956. A Pure Theory of Local Public Expenditures, *Journal of Political Economy* 64: 416–24.

West, D.M. 2008. Improving Technology Utilization in Electronic Government around the World, Washington D.C.: Brookings Institute.

Chapter 2 |

Evolution of Decentralization in Korea: From Intergovernmental Relations Perspectives

Soon Eun Kim

Introduction

Korea, in particular up to 2004, has been characterized by a high level of centralization since the Korean Dynasty due to, presumably, several reasons including an identical language across the country, ethnic homogeneity, and a relatively small territorial jurisdiction (Choi and Wright, 2004). The strong centralized political-administrative system has been a major feature of Korea for a long time, ever since Korean people have struggled for decentralization.

The purpose of this chapter is to analyze historical developments and describe the major characteristics of intergovernmental relations in Korea since 1948. The major features of intergovernmental relations in Korea, presumably, can be captured according to the historical occasions which had occurred in the past. Korea has its unique features as well as universal ones from which other countries might learn.

Several conceptual frameworks have been used to analyze intergovernmental relations of decentralization of different countries (Kim, 2008). Because features of intergovernmental relations are not identical from one country to another, different conceptual frameworks have been proposed by different scholars.

Typical frameworks of intergovernmental relations which have been quoted frequently are those deeply associated with Japan, the United Kingdom, and the United States. Professor Muramatsu (2000, 2001) has come up with two different conceptual frameworks in explaining the intergovernmental relations in Japan. One is a model which is categorized by the vertical control model and the mutually corresponding model. The other is a model which was borrowed from a manuscript by Kjelberg and Dente (1988): the autonomous model and the integrated model.

Wright (1988) explained American intergovernmental relations by way of three different models: the coordinate-authority model, dominant-authority model and overlapping model. Rhodes categorized four different models which are supposed to correspond to each different intergovernmental reality over time: the agency model, the stewardship model, the power dependency model and the partnership model.

Amagawa (1986) suggested that a level of decentralization including intergovernmental relations be categorized by two variables: centralization-decentralization and integration-separation. The former is related to the degree governmental authorities and powers are concentrated at the level of the central government, while the latter is associated with how much governmental authorities and powers overlap between different levels of governments. This study is dependent upon professor Amagawa's model to describe the different periods of intergovernmental relations in Korea.

Historical Developments of Intergovernmental Relations

Establishment of Decentralization: 1948–1960

This period can be characterized by trial and error in relation to local autonomy in Korea. As mentioned above, for the first time, a modern political system which included local autonomy was created after the 36 year Japanese colonial period and three year American military government period.

The constitution in 1948 contained two articles related to local autonomy which were, in sum, supposed to promote local autonomy in Korea under the law and ordinances made by the central government. Even though two articles which mandated local autonomy in Korea were not sufficient enough to guarantee a high level of local autonomy in Korea from a theoretical perspective the constitutional mandate itself was assessed as a historic institutional provision for establishment of local autonomy.

The Local Autonomy Act (hereinafter referred to as LAA) in 1949 contained provisions which functioned as a basis for creating a framework for local autonomy. In a word, not only elements of the continental "institutional autonomy" but also figures of the Anglo-American "citizen autonomy" were combined in the LAA of 1949 according to the constitutional mandate (Koo, 1990).

Main characteristics of the Anglo-American "citizen autonomy" are supposed to be associated with the sovereignty of local residents while the agency-delegated functions are supposed to be related to the continental law system which presupposes that the central government, the only entity of sovereignty, delegates its power to local entities. The LAA of 1949 contained basic provisions regarding the rights and duties of local residents, the organization and power of local councils, the formation of local executive and local finance, etc.

In particular, the LAA of 1949 adopted the two-tier system of local government: Seoul Metropolitan City and provinces as the upper-tier local government and, cities, towns and townships as the lower-tier local government. The upper-tier local governments were subject to the direct control of the central government while the lower-tier local governments were under the upper-tier local government's control.

Not only the upper-tier local governments but the lower-tier local governments were composed on the basis of the principle of the separation of power, that is, the mayor-council plan. Thus, the chief executives of the upper-tier local governments were supposed to be appointed by the president while the councils of the lower-tier local governments were supposed to elect the chief executives. The members of local councils were supposed to be elected by the public.

The lower-tier local governments were supposed to operate on the basis of the principle of checks and balances. The local councils of the lower-tier local governments were able to resolve non-confidence in local executives while local executives were empowered to disband local councils.

The level of autonomy according the LAA of 1949 was very low. The executives of the upper-tier local governments who were supposed to control the lower-tier local governments were appointed by the central government. In addition, the organization of Seoul Metropolitan City and provinces consisted of not only national public officials but local public officials too. The managerial level and above alike were recruited by national public officials. As far as the agency-delegated functions, the local governments functioned as an agent of the central government instead of local governing bodies.

The legislative power of local councils was granted to a limited extent. The degree of local legislative power fell within the law and ordinances. Furthermore, the legislative power among local councils was considerably different between metropolitan cities, including Seoul Special City, and other cities and towns.

To make matters worse, President Rhee succeeded in making several amendments of LAA in order to expand his political power. As a matter of fact, President Rhee held an unfavorable opinion of local autonomy and decentralization. From a development perspective of local autonomy, as a result, several amendments made in this period resulted in cancellation of the direct election system of lower-tier local governments. Instead all local executives were supposed to be appointed by the central government.

The phase 1 of local autonomy in this period can be assessed in two ways. First of all, the period is able to be evaluated as historic because of the establishment of local autonomy in Korea for the first time. But, this period can be also characterized by the deterioration, disruption and a drastic development of local autonomy or decentralization.

The Second Republic was a result of student revolution started in 1960. The constitution of the second republic stipulated the terms of local autonomy in a better way than the first republic's constitution. The constitution of the second republic provided that the chief executives of the lower-tier local governments should be elected by the public. On the basis of the constitution the second republic made more democratic amendments to the LAA in 1960. Not only members of local councils but also all local executives were supposed to be elected in an election.

It appears that five amendments of LAA during this period had been made for not improving the system of local governments on a trial and error basis; rather the central government had made five revisions of LAA because of political reasons. That is, the system of local governments in this period had been taken advantage of by the Rhee Administration which was intent on strengthening its political power.

The first period analyzed above was characterized by the establishment of a modern local autonomy system. The national goal of the first period was to make the country politically stable and to establish effective governance (Choi and Wright, 2004). To this end, a strongly centralized system remained. A high level of central supervision and control over local governments was legislated in the LAA of 1949.

Even though chief executives of the lower-tier governments were elected, those of the upper-tier local governments were appointed by the central government. Agency-delegated functions made local governments subservient to the central government. Implementation of agency-delegated functions by local governments should be handled under the central directives and mandates. In addition, the central government could either call off or suspend administrative actions taken by local governments which were assumed as illegal or irrational. The central government could also request local councils to call for a vote of no confidence of elected local chief executives who were judged as inappropriate for their jobs.

Even though public election of local chief executives was expanded to that of upper-tier local government in the LAA of 1960, the system of supervision and control of local governments by the central government remained unchanged.

The major circumstances of the first period were featured as ideological antagonisms between political parties, social disorder and instability of the political situation which called for a highly centralized political-administrative system even though the first and the second republic tried to promote local autonomy. In addition, implementation of national functions by local governments under the legal framework of agency-delegated functions made local governments agents of the central government. As a result, the central government and local governments worked closely to carry out public policies in a highly centralized system.

Centralization: 1961–1979

General Park's military coup in 1961 was a historic event for Korea's political system, particularly for intergovernmental relations between the central government and local governments. First of all, the Provisional Measure for Local Autonomy promulgated in 1961 disbanded local governments by suspending local autonomy in Korea.

The military government succeeded in fortifying the power of the central government under the premise of national security, social order and economic development, by dismantling local governments. Several specific measures were taken in order to improve the efficiency of the governmental system.

The first measure was related to the structure of local governments. The lower-tier local governments under the previous republic, Eup (towns) and Myun (townships), were amalgamated into autonomous political entities, Gun (counties). The autonomous power of local governments was retracted and all resolutions of local councils had to be approved by the higher levels of government. The resolutions of the upper-tier local councils were to be approved by the central government while those of the lower-tier local councils were to be approved by chief executives of the upper-tier local governments. Seoul Metropolitan Government was to operate under the direct control of the central government.

Subsequently, the constitution of the Third Republic amended that of the Second Republic by deleting the clause related to the election of the local executives of lower-tier local governments. The local autonomy in Korea was suspended up to the moment of reunification of the Korean peninsula according the constitution of the Third and Fourth Republic.

Park's Administration's policy goal had concentrated on economic development, by way of improved governmental efficiency and social order against the North Korean military threats which, either in sum or separately, functioned as a basis for interrupting and banning local autonomy in Korea. During this period local governments had not played a constructive role in political democracy.

Instead of dismantling local governments, the Park Administration streamlined local administration in terms of allowing central government to appoint all local executives at both the lower-tier and upper-tier of the local administrative systems while local elections of local councils were delayed up to the reunification of the Korean peninsula. Most appointed local chief executives of the local administrative system had abided by directives and mandates made by the central government. Most appointed local executives had not paid considerable attention to local residents' preferences. In addition, the streamlining of the local administrative system had been strengthened by dispatching national public officials to higher positions in the local administrative entities. The Ministry of Home Affairs (now "Ministry of Administration and Security") had served the role of local councils in terms of approving all resolutions as well as the budget of the local administrative entities. In a word, local administration had been under very strict supervision of the central government. It seems that local governments in this period had served only as agencies of the central government which merely implemented central policies, in particular, economic policies.

From a perspective of intergovernmental relations this period was characterized by a higher level of centralization. There were no local governments which existed as political entities at the local level but instead had served as only local administrative entities which functioned as agents of the central government.

The emphasis on efficiency and streamlining of local administrative entities by the Park Administration resulted in sacrifices of local autonomy and democracy which were based on local diversity and openness. This is one of the reasons why many people in numerous demonstrations argued for the implementation of local autonomy in order to improve Korean democracy. Unlike the case of Japan, demands for local autonomy in Korea have been deeply related to democratization in Korea.

The Third Period of 1980–1990

Since the Fifth Republic was established in 1980 two constitutional amendments were made. Even though articles about local autonomy in two amended constitutions were identical to the constitution of the Fourth Republic, restrictions on the timing for restoring local autonomy were slightly changed from the reunification of the Korean peninsula to the financial self-sufficiency of local governments. On the basis of the financial circumstances of local governments the gradual and partial transition towards local autonomy was expected under the Chun Administration.

The subsequent Roh Tae Woo Administration faced a political deadlock due to a lack of legitimacy of the military regime situation. Mass demonstrations in 1987 for democratization in Korea resulted in the historical "Declaration of Democratization in 1987" in which President Roh, designated successor of the president Chun, expressed his intent to restore the role of local autonomy in the near future. That is, the president Roh announced a public commitment to reinstate nation-wide local autonomy. As a result, restrictions on the timing for re-installation of local autonomy were removed not only in the constitution but also the LAA in 1988.

In particular, the revised LAA of 1988 functioned as a cornerstone for restoring local autonomy in Korea. It stipulated election days by stating that the election of lower-tier local councils should be carried out within one year and that of upper-tier local councils be conducted within two years.

The LAA of 1988 regulated the structure, organization, and the tier system of local governments. The chief executives of local governments were supposed to be appointed by the central government while members of local councils were supposed to be elected according the schedule mentioned above.

The LAA of 1988 adopted a two-tier system, including the Seoul Special City, Metropolitan Cities under the direct control of the central government, and provinces as the upper-tier local governments; and city, county, and autonomous boroughs within metropolitan cities as the lower-tier local governments. It also made an attempt to specify the governmental functions between the central government and local governments.

Decentralization Reform: The Fourth Period of 1991–President Noh

Step 1: 1991–before 2002

The year of 1991 was meaningful because the elections of members of local councils were carried out for the first time since 1961. Elections for local councilmen in 1991 and those for local chief executives in 1995 were obviously a turning point for inter-governmental relations in Korea. Local elected officials started to demand a high level of decentralization and the central government promised to carry out decentralization reforms in 1990s. Thus even though chief executives of local governments continued to be appointed by the central government the creation of elected local councils was significant enough to initiate gradual increases in local autonomy.

In line with the election of local councils the central government set up the Joint Council for Devolution whose function was to deliberate on governmental functions and authorities between the central government and local governments. The Council reviewed 3,701 functions of the central government for seven years and recommended that 2,008 functions of the central government be devolved to local governments (the Devolution Promotion Commission, 2001). However, only 1,639 functions were devolved to local governments. This was due to the fact that decisions of the Commission had no binding authority over relevant agencies (Kim, 2001).

It was in 1995 when full-scale local autonomy in Korea was initiated from a formal perspective since both chief executives of local government and members of local councils were elected by local residents. In order for members of local councils to be able to collect materials and study local governmental affairs they were granted monthly stipends

By way amending the LAA in 1999 citizen participation was strengthened because it was deemed a useful tool for monitoring and supervising matters and affairs of elected local officials, including local chief executives and members of local councils. A formal structural arrangement of local governments was completed in 1995; however, full-fledged local autonomy had been hindered due to restricted functions and authorities of local governments.

Although the Joint Council for Devolution of 1991 tried to devolve considerable functions of the central government to local governments, the results left something to be desired. In order to deal with this problem, the Kim Administration prepared an institutional basis for delegating many functions of the central government to local governments in a more effective way, that is, the 'Devolution Act of Central Administrative Functions to Local Governments' (hereinafter referred to as the "Devolution Act").

The Devolution Act provided major principles and fundamentals by which devolution efforts should be observed are as follows:

- Functions done by the central government and local governments ought to be devolved to local governments.
- Functions performed by both the upper-tier and the lower-tier local governments ought to be devolved to the lower-tier local governments.
- Functions related to one another ought to be devolved in aggregate to local governments
- Functions assigned to the central governments ought to be at the level of countrywide policies and national standardization.
- The Devolution Commission was created in order to promote

devolution of governmental functions to local governments.

Despite of the Devolution Act of the Kim Administration, its devolution efforts were assessed as unsuccessful by many policy experts of local autonomy (Kim, 2002, 2004). The Devolution Commission reviewed 3,374 functions for five years while the number of central functions which were deemed appropriate to be granted to local governments was not more than 1,090 (Kim, 2001; Hong, 2003).

During this period it was certain that local autonomy had been improved step-by-step in terms of increasing the level of local administrators' capability and creating a higher level of citizen participation. Nonetheless, in comparison with democratically well developed countries like the United States and Japan, etc., the level of local autonomy in Korea was assessed as not high enough (Kim, 2004).

In particular, it had been realized that de jure local autonomy was one thing, and de facto local autonomy was another. That is, since 1991, as mentioned above considerable efforts had been taken in order to realign governmental functions between the central government and local governments. Such issues as reinstating local autonomy, many central functions devolved to local governments, a high level of citizen participation and an increased level of monthly allowances to members of local councils, etc. are too misleading if one is to understand the circumstances of intergovernmental relations in Korea.

Although many institutional aspects had been improved for promoting local autonomy, monitoring and supervision of local governments by the central government had been confined by a framework made in 1949. From the perspective of intergovernmental relations, it is suggested that the central government keep local governments from imposing strong control and thus closely monitors the local governments. This is to say that it has been suggested local governments be granted a high level of flexibility in carrying out proper affairs of local governments or agency-deleted functions of the central government.

In this view, the central government has exercised a high level of supervision over local governments. Since the enactment of the LAA in 1949 amendments added to the LAA attempted to reduce the level of supervision and monitoring done by the central government of local governments. However the fact remains that local administration's implementation policies and management of local affairs has been under very strong central supervision. In particular, central government's monitoring and supervision of local governments has stood out in areas where centrally performed functions have been delegated. This supervision is done in particular by the central government delegating agency functions and dispatching personnel to local governments.

Intergovernmental relations have been strongly dominated by the central government thanks to money grants from the central government to local governments. Consequently the fiscal power of local governments has been generally low. Only 20 percent of the revenue of local governments has come from local taxes. In addition, the fiscal power of local governments has been diverse not only between the metropolitan areas and non-metropolitan areas but also between the capital area and non-capital regions.

The central institutions in Korea used to monitor and supervise local governments have been considerably wide open, including legislative, executive, and judicial devices (Lee, 2007). Most central institutions used to closely monitor and supervise local governments and have been coercive rather than suggestive or non-power oriented.

Step 2: 2003–Present

Not only in light of Korea's centralized system but also due globalization and decentralization trends in the 1980s, the Noh Administration inaugurated in 2003 announced a road map for a comprehensive decentralization reforms (Kim, 2003). Throughout the presidential campaign in 2002, presidential candidate Noh's pledges related to decentralization in Korea were a hot issue. Among other things, administrative decentralization and establishment of a new administrative capital were very controversial. After Noh won the presidential election, he announced a public commitment to carry out decentralization reform, including administrative decentralization and the establishment of a new administrative capital.

Noh's decentralization reform plan was based on basic statistics in association with public administration, including an allocation ratio of governmental affairs between the central and local governments, a ratio of revenue between the national and the local tax, and governing capability of local governments in terms of levels of citizen participation and administrative capacity of groups involved in local administration (Kim, 2004).

Governmental affairs were concentrated at the level of the central government in terms of 76 percent of all governmental functions while local governments were granted with 24 percent of all governmental affairs. National total revenue consisted of only 23.3 percent coming from local taxes and 76.7 percent from national taxes. Additionally the level of citizen participation was low while administrative capacity of groups involved in local affair was insufficient.

The reform plan consisted of seven major parts, including realigning authority between the central and local government, improving fiscal decentralization, promoting administrative independence of local governments, activating local legislation and improving election systems, improving the accountability of local governments, activating civil society and establishing cooperative intergovernmental relationships (Presidential Committee on Government Innovation and Decentralization, 2007). The road map was supposed to be implemented on the basis of three fundamental principles, including the principle of first decentralization and subsequent complementation, the principle of subsidiarity, and the principle of comprehensiveness, which stands for devolution of governmental affairs concerned with one another (Kim, 2004).

As a means of realigning authority between the central and local governments, many specific actions were taken, including legislation of Special Decentralization in 2003, the establishment of Jeju Island as a Special Self-governing Government, an amendment to the local autonomous educational system, the introduction of local policy systems, and the streamlining of local special administration agencies. The legislation of Special Decentralization in 2003 outlined the aims of the law, its fundamental decentralization philosophy, its linkage with other laws, duties and roles of the central government and local governments, and the principles of subsidiarity and comprehensive and inclusive devolution.

Jeju Island is removed from the Korean peninsula and possesses many geographical distinctions. In regards to its geographic characteristics the Noh Administration aimed to grant a higher level of autonomy to Jeju Island when compared to other regions. As a result, two special acts with respect to the establishment of Jeju's Special Self-governing Government and International Free City were passed in 2006 delegating the island more than 1,200 exceptional regulatory powers. In comparison with other local governments, Jeju's Special Self-governing Government is empowered to exercise a higher level of flexibility in carrying local administration in order to create an international free city.

Even though education is the most important concern for citizens of Korea, local educational administration and the local general administration in Korea had been operated separately without any connection.

To address problems with the local educational system, the Roh Moo-hyun Administration improved connections between the local educational administrations and local general administrations by having local educational committees operate as a component of the standing committees of local councils. In addition, both members of the educational committees and superintendents are supposed to be elected by the local residents.

Considerable efforts to establish a local police system had been taken by the Kim Dae-Jung Administration, which had put a high priority on policy related to police reform, but his efforts resulted in failure. Consequently the local police reform project was transferred to the Noh Administration which designated it as one of the core items of the administration's decentralization reform. Nonetheless, full-scale implementation of the local police system was not achieved; instead the local police system was introduced only in Jeju Special Self-governing Government.

The central government in Korea was privy to two different ways in carrying out national policies. The LAA has allowed the central government to commission its duties to the chief executives of local governments according to the continental legal convention. Another option for carrying out policy is for the central government to create its own local agencies under the Government Organization Act just in case it's commissioning of its duties to the chief executive of local government is not proper on the basis of a division of labor or special status. As a result, many central departments have established their local agencies which, presumably, have functioned as a tool in hindering comprehensive local administration.

Streamlining of the special local agencies of the central governments which were created by the central government and are supposed to implement national policies has been a core item of decentralization reform since the 1990s. Despite the high priority of reform, the reform plan of the special local agencies of the central governments had not been realized due to, not only considerable opposition from its interest groups, but also resistant attitudes of the central departments concerned.

Under the Noh Administration six central departments decided to transfer duties of their special local agencies to the Jeju Special Self-governing Government, including those of Jeju Local Land Administration Agency, the Jeju Environmental Agency, the Jeju branch office of the Gwangju Local Labor Agency, the Jeju Local Labor Commission, Jeju Regional Maritime and Fisheries Agency, the Jeju Welfare Agency, and the Jeju Local Small and Medium-sized Enterprises Agency.

In order to promote local administrative independence of local governments several efforts were taken in terms of strengthening local flexibility and improving local governments' personnel system. Governing capability was cited as a factor which can facilitate decentralization reform because local governments can successfully manage authorities and powers granted to them by the central government.

Towards improving governing capability of local governments the central government granted them a higher level of organizational autonomy by changing the standard quota system into the total labor cost system and improving the fair personnel management system in terms of increasing the number of the local personnel commission from "five to seven" to "seven to nine."

In order to increase the capability of local legislation and improve the local election system, several projects were under consideration. Presumably, vitality of local autonomy is deeply associated with democracy. Local councils, in particular, are supposed to be key players who are involved in local democratic politics. As a result, policy expertise and the local election system of local councils have been pinpointed as factors which should be ameliorated in the near future.

Towards this end, the system of the expert advisers was introduced. The amendment of the local election system resulted in deterioration of local politics due to the fact that newly introduced party nominations of members of lower-tier local councils functioned as a factor which made local politics dependent on central politics.

For the purpose of activating civil society local referendums, recall, and payer's suit were introduced step by step. The Local Referendum Act was legislated in 2005 after which several decision making methods involved in critical issues were addressed by the local referenda. The local recall had functioned as a tool by which local residents could prevent local elected officials from pursuing inappropriate policies. The tax payers' suit functioned as a tool which ameliorated the transparency and accountability of local administration.

Several efforts, in order to improve fiscal decentralization, were taken in terms of the transfer of central government's functions and financial resources to local governments, promotion of national subsidy management, establishment of a balanced national development special account, and improvement of local transferred tax system.

The ratio of general revenue sharing of had been incrementally increased up to 19 percent while the special shared tax system was amended. In particular, the shared tax for decentralization was introduced and a balanced regional development special account was established.

Characteristics of the Korean Experience of Decentralization

On the basis of an axis (variable) of integration-separation which means by ways in which allocation of governmental functions and authorities are supposed to be performed, and another axis of centralization-decentralization which represents how allocation of governmental authorities are supposed to be done, Korea is characterized by a model of centralization-integration. The historical analyses of the previous sections indicate that the essential features of intergovernmental relations in Korea can be explained by a model of centralization-integration despite of several attempts to devolve central functions and power to local government in each period mentioned above.

A High Level of Centralization

After six decades of trial and experimentation, local autonomy in Korea, on the whole, has remained with a high level of centralization. Additionally the practice of agency-delegated functions initiated during the time of Japanese Colony have been retained up to now. There have been many arguments against the agency-delegated functions as a means of promoting decentralization; however, local governments have functioned as a local agent of the central government as far as the agency-delegated functions are concerned. 70 percent of functions which local governments are supposed to carry out are related to the agency-delegated functions.

Intergovernmental relations between the central government and local governments feature administrative linkages between the central government and local governments. From long ago, even in the Chosun Dynasty outstanding linkage between the central government and local governments has been a method of administrative control over local governments by the central government in terms of authoritative interpretations of regulations, and directives and mandates issued by central bureaucrats.

The Central government's bureaucratic supervision over local governments has been carried out by way of appointing the central government's high officials to the local governments' management positions. Usually, higher level officials of the Ministry of Administration and Security have been appointed to key positions of upper-tier local governments. The central government has influenced local governments' affairs through these higher ranking officials who were transferred to local governments. The central bureaucratic domination over local governments has functioned as a basis for describing Korean intergovernmental relations in terms of the vertical administrative control model.

The third element which has characterized intergovernmental relations in Korea used to be financial flows from the central government and local governments. The local revenue from local taxes are supposed to make up 20 percent of local expenditures. However, local governments are supposed to spend over 50 percent of total national income, which means that local governments cannot operate without grants-in-aid by the central government.

The central government has imposed considerable influence

over local governments by different kinds of grants-in-aid, including general revenue sharing, block grants, and categorical grants-in-aid. The system of the grants-in-aid and that of central approval of loans by local governments have functioned as a foundation for supervising and monitoring local governments.

In other words, local government officials have tried to contact and persuade central officials responsible for the transfer of national funds to local governments through various ways available to them and based on their necessities and sense of urgency. The financial framework of local governments in Korea has been an important factor in determining the centralized administrative system.

Democratization and Local Autonomy

Intergovernmental relations in Korea have been deeply related to democratization and globalization which has had an impact on changing Korean governmental roles, and in particular, those of the central government. In other words, decentralization reform and local autonomy has had considerable impact on intergovernmental relations in Korea and can be closely associated with democratization movements since the 1970s. Decentralization reform in Korea has also been a governmental policy used to cope with a new international environment, that is, globalization which made roles of local governments more significant than before.

As analyzed above, since 1961 when local autonomy was suspended due to the May 16th military coup of that year, restoring of local autonomy had been one of many items called for when addressing the topic of democratization of the political system in Korea. Presidential nominee Roh declared a plan for democratization in Korea in 1987, called as "Declaration of Democratization," in which the reinstallation of local autonomy was included.

In addition, the public commitment made by president Roh represented an historic moment in which preparatory actions for the restoration of local autonomy started to take place. Amendments to the Constitution and LAA were followed by the Declaration of Democratization.

The challenge of globalization has had considerable influence over decentralization reforms and local autonomy which have eventually reshaped intergovernmental relations in Korea. Guided by the ideology of small central government, the decentralization movement had proliferated globally since 1980. The international trend of decentralization was supposed to culminate in localization.

Central-local relations in Korea since the 1980s have already revealed an international trend toward decentralization which was also can be found in Japan and other European countries. The major concern with decentralization has been restructuring intergovernmental relations in harmony with the changing international environment.

Eventually, as analyzed in the above, former president Noh announced a public commitment to carry out comprehensive decentralization reform and published a decentralization road map for it. Noh's administration had tried to devolve many central powers to local governments in a progressive manner. In relation to the decentralization reforms of the Noh administration, one issue in particular deserves discussing, that is, the relations between decentralization and regional balanced development which is discussed in the next section.

Decentralization and Regional Balanced Development

Two major policies which were listed by the Roh Administration as being of high priority reform which were decentralization and regional balanced development. As I discussed above, the political and administrative system in Korea has been highly centralized and several negative side effects have occurred since the 1970s. One of them is considerable discrepancy between regions, in particular, between the capital region and other regions. Almost half of Korean population lives in the Capital region and 70 percent of major governmental and educational, and cultural infrastructures are located in the Capital region.

This represented a real basis for adopting decentralization and regional balanced development policies by the Noh administration simultaneously. Due to the innate policy nature of decentralization and regional balanced development there have been considerable controversies about how to proceed with decentralization and regional balanced development policies in a harmoniously.

Despite many controversies regarding the relationships between decentralization and regional balanced development the Noh administration chose to proceed with two decentralization and regional balanced development policies at the same time.

The method of regional balanced development of the Noh administration consisted of three major elements: devolution of the central governmental power to the local governments, delocalization of the central governmental agencies to regions other than the capital area, and scattering of public corporations in a similar fashion. That is, as far as regional balanced development was concerned, decentralization was constituted as an element of the regional balanced development policy.

It was presumed there would be no conflicts or friction during the devolution of governmental powers, dispersion of governmental agencies, and scattering of companies. However, in the implementation process of both the decentralization and regional balanced development policies, the innate nature of decentralization and regional balanced development was becoming clear.

It became clear that decentralization policy is superficially agreed upon by members concerned in simply because it is relatively easy for all local governments to agree upon it. Even local governments in the capital region do not object to decentralization policies.

However, regional balanced development is inherently creates conflict among partners concerned because it is comparatively difficult to build a consensus. There used to be big differences between regions in respect to regional balanced development policies and fierce conflicts between regions regarding the dispersion of governmental agencies and scattering of companies. In particular, there used to be no consensus between local governments in the capital region and other local governments. As a result, the central government had played a pivotal role in dispersing governmental agencies and scattering public corporations all over the country.

The decentralization policy and regional balanced development policies can work in favor of the opposite direction; decentralization can seek to pit local governments against each other for the sake of their development, which can result in increasing the gaps among regions, despite regional balanced development policy's aims of equalizing the living standards across the country. Curiously local governments had been more interested in regional balanced development policies which were supposed to be accompanied by financial support than decentralization policies which were supposed to grant local governments with more discretion and flexibility.

Conclusion

This is an analysis regarding the intergovernmental relations in Korea since 1948. This analysis shows that the intergovernmental relations in Korea have changed over different periods as a result of different legal and institutional environments. In addition, the intergovernmental relations in Korea have been influenced by the international atmosphere too.

Considerable efforts have been taken to make intergovernmental relations in Korea decentralized politically and administratively. It is evident that the political democratization movements accompanied decentralization along with other democratization reforms. Therefore power politics perspectives are relevant when attempting to understand the evolution of intergovernmental relations in Korea. Unlike the United States and other countries, financial crisis and efficiency were not the determinant factors for the decentralization reforms in Korea.

Nonetheless, the intergovernmental relations in Korea are characterized by a high level of centralization in terms of supervision and monitoring by the central government of local governments and the system of financial grants-in-aid, etc. Through this close relationship, Korea managed to maintain solid integration among regions. This is the reason why the decentralists have never been satisfied with actual decentralization reforms and criticize the bureaucratic control of the central government of the local governments regardless of the reforms measures. In this sense Korea has never experienced an extreme type of decentralization akin to the federal system.

Finally, it is very interesting to recognize that local governments in Korea are more interested in regional balanced development policies with central financial aid than decentralization policies with a higher level of local discretion and flexibility. It seems that local governments would enjoy central financial aid without accountability while decentralization is supposed to require a higher degree of accountability for local governments. This local attitude might lead to local moral hazards however.

References

Presidential Committee on Government Innovation and Decentralization. 2007. Innovation and Decentralization of Korean Government, Seoul: Presidential Committee on Government Innovation and Decentralization.

The Devolution Promotion Commission. 2001. Devolution Promotion Circumstances, http://www.dpla.go.kr.

Amagawa, H. 1986. Ideas of Reform: Doshusei. Japanese Local Government, Tokyo: Tokyo National University Press.

Choi, Y. and D., Wright. 2004. Intergovernmental Relation (IGR) in Korea and Japan: Phases, Patters, and Progress toward Decentralization (Local Autonomy) in a Trans-pacific Context, *International Review of Public Administration* 9(1): 1–22.

Hong, J. 2003. Problems and Alternatives of Devolution Efforts of Central Functions, http://www.dpla.go.kr.

Kjelberg, F. and D., Dente. eds. 1988. The Dynamics of Institutional Change: Local Government Reorganization in Western Democracies, London: Sage Publications.

Kim, S. 2001. Characteristics and Tasks of Decentralization in Korea: A Comparative Study of Decentralization among Japan, U.K. and Korea, *Korean Society and Administration Review* 12(2): 57–75.

_______. 2002. An Evaluation of Decentralization Reform Plan of the Participation Government, *Korean Journal of Local Government Studies* 7(2): 113–33.

_______. 2004. Governmental Innovation and Decentralization Reform, *Local Government Studies Review* 8(1): 151–76.

_______. 2008. Intergovernmental Relations in Korea. In Korean Association for Local Autonomy Studies, ed. *Understanding of Korea Local Autonomy* Seoul: Parkyoungsa.

Koo, B. 1990. New Constitution, Seoul: Parkyoungsa. Lee, K. 2007.

Muramatsu, M. 2001. Intergovernmental Relations in Japan: Models and Perspective, World Bank Institute.

_______. and F., Iqbal. 2000. Understanding Japanese Intergovernmental Relations: Perspectives, Models and Salient Cha-

racteristics, In M. Muramatsu, ed. *Japanese Intergovernmental Relations* Tokyo.
Wright, D. 1988. Understanding Intergovernmental Relations, 3rd ed. Pacific Grove: Brooks/Cole Publishing Company.

Part II

Economic Development

Chapter 3 |

Decentralization and Economic Development

TOBIN IM AND WONHYUK CHO

Introduction

Many countries around the world, including developing countries, are decentralizing fiscal, political, and administrative responsibilities by introducing local elections as well as by devolving central power to local authorities. Many reformers blindly support the idea that decentralization, by counterbalancing central government's excessive power, will increase the efficiency of political machinery and result in economic growth. Others believe that decentralization will help an authoritative regime transform into democratic one. Whatever the political intentions, decentralization can significantly affect resource mobilization and allocation and ultimately macroeconomic stability and economic growth (Iimi, 2005; Lin and Liu 2000; Litvack, Ahmad and Bird 1998; Martinez-Vazquez and McNab, 2003).

Decentralization is also an expressed goal of the national governments of many developing countries and also constitutes part of their economic development strategy (Bahl and Linn, 1994). Decentralization has been experimented with in a number of developing and transitioning economies in Latin America, Africa and Asia (Bardhan, 2002). Consequently reforms in favor of decentralization have been of major concern for developing countries, international development communities and researchers for last several decades (Jutting et al., 2004).

Supposing the relationship between the United States' or German economy and their decentralized system, decentralization is widely believed to promise a range of benefits, and the centralized states seem to have lost a great deal of legitimacy (Bardhan, 2002; 185). Reformers dissatisfied with the results of centralized economic planning have turned to decentralization to break the grip of central government and induce broader participation in democratic governance (Olowu, 2000; Smoke, 1994; Wunsch and Olowu; 1990). Decentralization is regarded as a way of making government more responsive and efficient, so developing countries are adopting it as a way of solving problems such as inefficient and ineffective administration and low levels of economic growth (Bird, 1993). Many researchers and practitioners around the world have supported these benefits. Free-market economists have emphasized reducing the power of the overextended state through decentralization, while postmodernist, multicultural advocates, grassroots environmental activists and supporters of indigenous people have upheld the assignment of control to local self-governing communities (Bardhan, 2002;, 186).

This chapter raises a fundamental question about the cause and effect relationship between decentralization and economic growth. For instance, Korea accomplished unprecedented rapid economic growth for the last several decades although its governance structure was, at least seemingly, highly centralized. So it is questionable whether decentralization is in fact a proper policy prescription for economic development in developing countries. Within this context, this study tries to examine the question of whether centralized governance during the developmental period contributed to its economic development. This is particularly of great importance for countries whose main concern is economic development and are consequently pursuing decentralization.

This chapter will, however, focus more on the indirect impact of decentralization on economic growth rather than the direct relationship on which previous empirical studies have focused. There are many factors that significantly affect economic development, so the direct relationship between decentralization and economic development can be much less relevant than indirect factors closely related to decentralization. According to our literature review on this subject, major mediating variables between decentralization and economic growth are economic efficiency, corruption, macroeconomic instability, elite capture and administrative capacity.

Theoretical Perspectives and Empirical Evidence

Theoretical Perspectives

Many studies that support decentralization are implicitly or explicitly inspired by Tiebout (1956) and Oates (1972, 1999). Tiebout's model, called "voting with feet," assumes that individuals are fully mobile and will move to the community where their preferences are best satisfied, which will result in competition among local governments. Oates (1972, 1999) assumed that local governments were better positioned than the central government to deliver public services to the citizen as a result of their information advantage. Oates (1993) and Martinez and McNab (2003, 1603–1606) studied the relationship between decentralization and economic growth, at least partly, inspired by the inference of these assumptions of economic efficiency. Economic efficiency here refers to a minimization of waste because public resources are allocated exactly and should be based on reflections of citizens' true needs. Increased efficiency will contribute economic growth.

There are mixed findings, however, about the effect of decentralization on economic growth, both in cross-country analyses and in studies within a single country. In other words, empirical studies do not prove consistently that decentralization is positively related to economic growth. Davoodi and Zou (1998) provided a simple endogenous growth model showing how the degree of fiscal decentralization affects the economic growth rate through a cross-country panel data set of 46 developed and developing countries from 1970 to 1989. They found a negative relationship between fiscal decentralization and growth in developing countries, and no relationship for developed countries. Zhang and Zou's (1998) study, based on annual data on 28 provinces in China from 1986 to 1992, revealed that a higher degree of fiscal decentralization was associated with lower regional economic growth in China. They argued that an increase in sub-national government-level expenditures cause a decline in the real growth rate of regional income. The key infrastructure projects, according to Zhang and Zou's (1998) study, may have a far more significant impact on economic growth across provinces than their counterparts in each province; the association between central government development spending and economic growth is positive and significant, while provincial governments' expenditure for development is negatively associated with economic growth.

These findings offer an important lesson for other developing countries and transitioning economies blindly pursuing fiscal decentralization. Since the 1970s, China has promoted fiscal reforms with the aim of decentralizing fiscal expenditures and ensuring the central government's role in the fiscal revenue side of things (World Bank, 2000). However, many scholars such as Ma (1995) and Zhang and Zou (1998) argue that fiscal decentralization in China was implemented too rapidly and too extensively. What is interesting is that this is not a simple problem which just concerns developing countries. Xie, Zou and Davoodi (1999) examined the relationship between fiscal decentralization and regional growth in the United States economy from 1948 to 1994. They interpreted the insignificant coefficients on subnational government expenditure shares as a policy implication that further decentralization in public spending is harmful to growth in the United States context.

On the contrary, there also exist several empirical studies supportive of a positive relationship between decentralization and growth. In the cross-country context, Huther and Shah (1998), though investigating a simple correlation, showed that fiscal decentralization is positively associated with quality of governance, which is presumed to accelerate economic development. Thiessen (2000) found a positive and direct relationship between decentralization and growth for panels of high-income, Western European, and middle-income countries. Akai and Sakata (2002) argued that they provided new evidence that fiscal decentralization contributes to economic growth, in contrast to previous studies that have denied such a contribution. They insisted that their new state-level data for the United States enables them to estimate the effect of fiscal decentralization more objectively than previously, because the data set exhibits little cultural, historical, or institutional variation. Lin and Liu (2000) investigated the effect of fiscal decentralization initiated in the mid 1980s in China on the growth rate of per capita GDP. They found that fiscal decentralization has made a significant contribution to economic growth, which is consistent with the hypothesis that fiscal decentralization can increase economic efficiency. In addition, they argued that rural reform, capital accumulation, and nonstate sector development were the key driving forces of economic growth in China over the past 20 years or so. They argued that, according to the data set, fiscal decentralization has raised the growth rate in China mainly by improving the efficiency of resource allocation rather than by inducing more investment. Iimi (2005), using the instrument variables technique with cross-country data for the period from 1997 to 2001, found that fiscal decentralization has a significant positive impact on per capita GDP growth. And it was argued that when the focus is placed on the latest information on the economic situation in the latter 1990s, decentralization, particularly in terms of fiscal expenditure, is instrumental in economic growth.

No matter what the results are in those studies, there are many methodological issues and problems in empirical studies testing the role of decentralization in economic growth (Martinez-Vazquez and McNab, 2003). One of the critical limitations of previous studies is that most of them focused on only one aspect of decentralization: fiscal decentralization, measured by the subnational share of total expenditure. Although it is clear that fiscal decentralization is an essential element of the decentralization process, subnational share in total expenditure cannot fully reflect the diverse and multidimensional processes of decentralization in different countries, and thus, fiscal decentralization has serious limitations when it comes to analyzing the relationship between decentralization and economic development. The decentralization reforms being implemented now in many developing countries are not just about fiscal decentralization however. For example, many developing countries decided to make local officials' positions elective. Further, the level of real decision-making power of elected local officials is different in each country.

One of many reasons that previous studies used subnational share in total expenditure as the only indicator of decentralization seems to be the fact that it is relatively easy to measure and convenient to analyze using statistical methods. But considering the limitations of this approach, the concept of decentralization will be categorized into several different aspects in the next part of this chapter to analyze the Korean experience of decentralization and economic development.

There are also many different ways to define economic growth or economic development, because it is in fact a very broad concept. Previous studies used either annual GDP growth or GDP per capita growth as an indicator of economic growth or development. Nevertheless, it is necessary to keep consistency in the case of the dependant variable so that it can be compared accurately with previous studies. Therefore the term 'economic growth' or 'economic development' in this study refers to the GDP growth rate.

Empirical Evidence

The methodology this study relies on is basically literature review and simple analysis of data. The availability of valid data constrains this study to include only 34 developing countries covering annual observations from 1970 to 2007. A time-series cross-section regression with a fixed effect model is used because the pooled

OLS models could be biased in several ways (Oakley, 1999). Based on the findings of the statistical tests, this chapter focuses on possible risks of decentralization which can do harm to the developing countries' economic growth. In particular, Korean decentralization experiences will be discussed in more detail.

Dependent variable, the countries' economic growths, is measured by each country's annual GDP growth rate which is regarded as the most widely used indicator among others to be representative for the country's wealth. The GDP data that this study uses is from World Development Indicator by the World Bank.

Fiscal decentralization was calculated based on IMF's Government Finance Statistics (GFS). We calculated the sub-national government's share of total spending with a ratio of local governments' total expenditure over central government's total expenditure.

For the political decentralization variable, Freedom House's index of "political rights" and "civil liberty," is used as an indicator. Although political rights and civil liberty do not perfectly reflect the political decentralization of local government, these indexes are valuable for capturing the degree of political decentralization (Iimi, 2005; 453). Iimi (2005) suggested that the political rights variable is expected to reflect the degree of political devolution at the municipal level, and additionally incorporated the political right variable as one of the major variables in the model of decentralization and economic growth.

As control variables, population growth rate and inflation rate are included; the reason that the number of control variables is very limited is because the data of developing countries has very limited level of availability. The data for population growth rates and inflation rates that this study used are from the World Development Indicator.

With these variables, the following regression model is estimated with a longitudinal data set.

$$y_{it} = x_{it}\beta + a_i + u_{it}$$

In the model, y_{it} is GDP growth rate where i is the country, t is the year, $\hat{\beta}$ is the vector of coefficients, x_{it} is a vector of independent variables, a_i is the individual effect and u_{it} is the error term.

The estimator is assumed to be as follows.

$$\hat{\beta} = \left[\sum_{i,t}^{I} \hat{x}_{it}{}'\hat{x}_{it}\right]^{-1}\left[\sum_{i,t}^{I} \hat{x}_{it}{}'\hat{y}_{it}\right]$$

And $\hat{x}_{it} = x_{it} - \bar{x}_{it}$ is the zero-mean independent variable, while $\hat{y}_{it} = y_{it} - \bar{y}_{it}$ is the zero-mean dependant variable.

This study chose the following 34 countries for the sample of developing countries. This sample includes all the countries of the category explained below as far as the reliable data sets are available.

> Albania, Armenia, Azerbaijan, Belarus, Bolivia, Brazil, Bulgaria, Chile, Colombia, Croatia, Dominican Republic, El Salvador, Georgia, Honduras, Iran, Kazakhstan, Latvia, Lithuania, Malaysia, Mauritius, Mexico, Moldova, Mongolia, Panama, Paraguay, Peru, Poland, Romania, Russia, Senegal, South Africa, Tajikistan, Thailand, Ukraine

Although the definition of the term 'developing county' itself has been controversial, this study sampled countries based on their wealth. World Bank's Income group definition divides economies according to 2007 GNI per capita calculated World Bank Atlas method. The groups are low income with USD 935 or less; lower middle income, USD 936–3,705 ; upper middle income, USD 3,706–11,455 ; and high income, USD 11,456 or more. This study considers countries with less than 11,455 dollars of GNI per capita as developing countries.

The most important finding is in relation to the developing countries because this group of countries can learn how and when to proceed with decentralization reforms as a strategy of development. In the regression result, there is a significant negative relationship between political decentralization and GDP growth rate at the 0.05 level and no relationship between fiscal decentralization and the GDP growth rate. While the Iimi's (2005) results show a positive impact of fiscal decentralization, Davoodi and Zou (1998) found that fiscal decentralization is negatively related to growth at the 10 percent level of significance. Contrary to the results of these two studies, statistically significant relationships between fiscal decentralization and growth are not observed in developing countries. Instead, political decentralization is found to be negatively related to growth in this study.

These results imply that fiscal and political decentralization which have been very widely adopted in developing countries can have unexpected negative effects on a countries' economic growth. More precisely, political decentralization reforms may seriously impact a country's economic development.

The case of Thailand's decentralization can help demonstrate the negative results of this relationship between unintended consequences of decentralization and economic growth. Thailand had maintained a highly centralized system, and its intergovernmental

Table 1. Regression Result

Dependent Variable: GDP Growth Rate			
Independent Variable	Fixed Effect Model		
	(1)	(2)	(3)
Constant	9.1668*** (3.2298)	9.1783*** (3.2303)	9.9748*** (3.1652)
Fiscal Decentralization	0.0253 (0.0518)	0.0217 (0.0519)	−0.0055 (0.0513)
Political Decentralization	−0.4851*** (0.1685)	−0.5383*** (0.1779)	−0.4492** (0.1766)
Population Growth Rate		−0.5321 (0.5682)	−0.2461 (0.5602)
Inflation Rate			−0.0028*** (0.0006)
R-Square	0.2023	0.2043	0.2251
F-Value	2.55 (<.0001)	2.57 (<.0001)	2.34 (0.0001)
Number of Countries	34	34	34
Length of Time Series	38	38	38

Notes: Statistically significant at * the 0.1 level, ** the 0.05 level, *** the 0.01 level. Figures on parenthesis are standard errors. *F*-value of fixed effect model refers to the result of *F*-test for no fixed effect.

relationship had changed little until the 1990s (Mutebi, 2004). The subnational government had no meaningful autonomy and even the wave of Thai decentralization reforms in the early 1990s were largely only concerned with a fiscal devolution initiative (Mutebi, 2004). However, the new constitution in 1997 brought fundamental changes to Thailand's political decentralization. Decentralization of power and promotion of local self-government were stated in the constitution, and autonomous powers in policy formulation, administration, finances and personnel management were granted to local governments (Mutebi, 2004). Local election of local councils and executive bodies were mandated, and the constitution provided local citizens with the right to recall votes and throw elected local officials deemed dishonest out of office (Mutebi, 2004). In addition to this new constitution, the Decentralization Act was enacted in 1999.

In contrast to the very active Thai economy in the late 1980s and early 1990s, the economic performance was not very good following this series of political decentralization initiatives; the five years' average GDP growth rate from 2001 to 2005 was 5.07 percent while the rate from 1990 to1994 was 9.00 percent.

Possible Risks of Decentralization: Mediating Factors

In contrast to the theoretical predictions made by the traditional view, there is great variation among practical results due to the countries' differing institutional environments and circumstances. Several possible risks of decentralization were suggested in previous studies, and developing countries are usually much more vulnerable to these dangers. These risks, if they occur, must directly or indirectly affect economic growth, which means that these factors play a moderating role between decentralization and economic development.

Corruption

Prud'homme (1995) argued theoretically, and supported with examples, that there are probably more opportunities for corruption at the local level. The logic behind these arguments is that first, local bureaucrats and politicians are likely to be more subject to pressing demands from local interest groups. Second, local officials usually have more discretionary powers than national decision makers. Banfield (1979) also argued that decentralized political systems are more corruptible, because the potential corrupter needs to influence only a segment of the government. Additionally in a fragmented system there are fewer centralized forces and agencies to enforce honesty. Bardhan and Mookherjee (2000) argued that countries where a greater share of public business is conducted at subnational levels would be more corrupt and less effective at providing public goods because interest groups may be more cohesive at the local level.

Empirically, Goldsmith (1999) argued that administrative centralization is associated with lower degrees of political corruption through a cross-country regression analysis using the Corruption Perceptions Index (CPI) released by Transparency International (TI). This study points out that federal or decentralized systems make it easier to hide corrupt practices. With the cross-country regression (using TI's and the World Bank's corruption indexes, with data on 154 countries), Treisman (2000a) argued that states with more tiers of government tend to have higher perceived corruption and may also do a worse job of providing public services. In a later study, he also found that federal states are more corrupt than unitary ones, using cross-country regressions with TI's CPI as the main dependent variable (Treisman, 2000b). He attributed this higher level of corruption in federal states to the collective action problem of subnational officials in deciding how much to extract bribes from businesses they have the power to regulate. According to Treisman, competition between autonomous levels of government to extract bribes leads to "'overgrazing" of the commons. Unitary states, in contrast, have more effective hierarchical control which enables central officials to limit the subnational officials' bribery to a more "reasonable" level. In this case, decentralizing political power and giving total autonomy to local governments in poor countries are likely to increase corruption among local employees.

Another argued benefit of hierarchical control which is supported by many studies is the belief that competition among different levels of government leads to a decrease in corruption (Breton, 1996; Weingast, 1995; Arikan, 2004; Fisman and Gatti, 2002). However, these studies did not consider the particularity of developing countries' political-administrative situations, or even the empirical tests which turned out to be insignificant (Arikan, 2004). Each country's different institutional and social settings could affect local governments' corruption levels tremendously. Shleifer and Vishny (1993) suggested a theoretical model which argued that not only nations with a highly centralized institutional structure but also those with a very decentralized structure may suffer less from the damaging effects of corruption than states with an intermediate level of institutional centralization. Brueckner (2000) analyzed the consequences of altering Tiebout's model, which claimed that decentralized provision of public goods allows for the better fulfillment of diverse individual demands, by including local corruption and tax evasion, which may exist in many developing countries, and the analysis showed that these forces limit the benefits of decentralization. Decentralization, according to Tanzi (2000), can be good only if proper institutional grounds are established, but these conditions for successful decentralization are often not in place, especially in developing countries.

Empirical cases support the hypothesis that decentralization in developing countries at least partly increases corruption. Fjeldstad (2001) found that fiscal administrations in many local authorities in Tanzania were highly corrupt, partly due to local officials' extreme degree of discretionary fiscal powers and poor (or nonexistent) monitoring from above. Mana (1999) examined the causes and characteristics of corruption at the provincial level in Papua New Guinea and argued that the decentralization reforms in Papua New Guinea in 1995 resulted in increased discretion among provincial governors as well as increased competition among NGOs, leading to enhanced pressure for corrupt practices. Also it is important to note that monitoring mechanisms of public bureaucrats are much weaker in low-income countries than others (Bardhan, 2002).

Macroeconomic Instability

Decentralization can affect the macroeconomic stability of a country which, in turn, influences economic growth. Since local governments have less incentive to consider the macroeconomic impact of their policies than central governments do, decentralization can have a negative impact on macroeconomic stability; especially in developing countries whose economic conditions are unstable (Hoffman, 1999). Decentralization can reduce the tax and expenditure base that the central government can use to carry out its stabilization functions, and poorly designed decentralization policies can create incentives for subnational governments to spend irresponsibly and unsustainably (Seddon, 1999).

Some countries, including Brazil and China, experienced macroeconomic problems when their tax bases were decentralized without a clear assignment of expenditures to the lower level of governments which receive the revenues (Hoffman, 1999, 89; Dillinger, 1997). The expansion of local government expenditure in Argentina, Brazil, Columbia, and Mexico undermined their central fiscal policies when subnational deficits resulted in a bailout by the national government, which made it more difficult for the central governments to control their budget deficits and stabilize inflation during the 1994 Latin American economic crisis (Dillinger, 1999).

Elite Capture

Bardhan and Mookherjee (2002) argued, inspired by the capture theory, that there is a tendency for services to be overprovided to local elites at the expense of non-elites. The extent of such inefficient and inequitable cross-subsidization depends on the extent of local capture and on the degree of fiscal autonomy that local governments enjoy. Therefore the effects that decentralization will bring depend upon the relative vulnerability of national and local governments to capture by influential interest groups, as well as on the existence of an appropriate set of political and economic institutions (Bardhan and Mookherjee, 1998, 1999).

Mani (2003) found that local government officials in less developed areas often wield power within the local community and use this power to manipulate information and development for the benefit of the particular group they belong to. In a similar context, Bardhan and Mookherjee (2000) argued that the relative proneness to capture local governments depends on a multitude of diverse factors. This study supports the Madisonian presumption that the degree of capture is highly correlated to the cohesiveness of interest groups and higher levels of voter ignorance at the local level. But they also identified a number of other determinants of capture that pull in different directions. These include the relative extent of electoral competition, electoral uncertainty, and the value of campaign funds in local and national elections. Other relevant factors include heterogeneity among local districts with respect to intra-district inequality, and different electoral systems at the two levels. The contrasting roles of these diverse factors suggest that the extent of relative capture at the local level may well turn out to be context and system specific.

Lack of Administrative Capacity in Local Government

Lack of institutional capacity of local government can be a serious problem, especially in developing countries. Local governments in developing countries generally lack the managerial, technical, and financial capacity to plan and implement policies and public services. Bardhan (2002) argued that decentralization literature typically assumes that different levels of government have similar levels of technical and administrative capacity, but this assumption is questionable, especially for developing countries. According to him, a central bureaucracy attracts better talent on account of an agglomeration of economies in attracting qualified people. This problem is especially severe in many developing countries where the quality of staff, including those handling basic tasks such as accounting and record–keeping, is very low at the local level (Bardhan, 2002; 189). Although it is assumed that local governments may know what to do, they may not know how to do it (Bird, 1993).

Mani (2003) stated several problems regarding local government's capacity in developing countries. Local governments in less developed regions' greatest problems can be found in the area of recruiting qualified personnel and a very weak managerial capacity.

Many developing countries are in a situation where central governments attract the most-qualified human resources while local governments function with less qualified personnel. Moreover, the private sector and multilateral and bilateral agencies engaged in development attract skilled staff away from government by offering higher salaries. Additionally motivation of staff is low because of frequent transfers and low salaries. In terms of skills, local government personnel tend to have poorer qualifications and less experience in generation and disbursement of resources for development. Furthermore, they lack sufficient skills in collaborative planning with NGOs and CBOs as well as in participatory planning with communities, lack the capacity to identify threats to development and target vulnerable populations, and have a limited mandate and capacity for conflict resolution.

The relationships among variables that this study presumes are summarized in Figure 1 below.

Figure 1. Schematic Relations among Variables

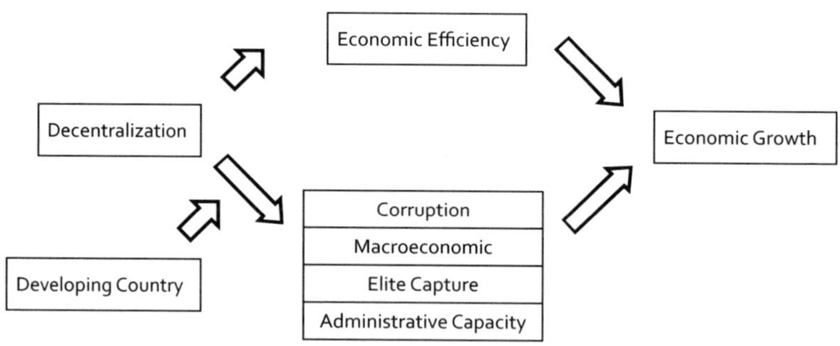

Decentralization and Economic Growth in Korea

The decentralization process in Korea can be categorized into three periods which are based on the existence of local elections: from 1948 to 1961, from 1962 to 1991, and after 1992. Korea started with a decentralized system, at least at the legal level, because the Constitution formed in 1948 after liberation clearly called for local autonomy and a Local Autonomy Act was enacted in 1949. The first local council election was held in 1952. However, this radical decentralization went through a great change after the military coup in 1961. Following the coup, local elections were never held, and mayors and governors as well as directors of local governments were bureaucrats appointed by the central government. Local elections finally resumed in 1991, thanks to the democratization movement. Local autonomy has steadily increased since then, which has been more or less successful from the viewpoint of participatory democracy.

However, closer examination of the Korean decentralization process is required; having local elections instead of centrally appointing local officials is just one of many aspects of decentralization—which include, as mentioned above, administrative, fiscal, political, and market aspects. Thus to fully understand the decentralization process of a country, one must view it from several dimensions. We will use Im's framework in our analysis, with its four models of decentralization: Centralization, Controlled Decentralization, Deconcentration, and Decentralization.

1948–1961: Controlled Decentralization Model

In this period, decentralization was attempted seemingly for the purpose of establishing a liberal democratic system in South Korea. The Local Autonomy Act of 1949 is widely accepted as the start of local self-government in Korea, and in 1952, local council elections were held.

However, local elections in this period had a somewhat different meaning from what we generally assume of decentralization. The true intention of introducing local elections at a time of poor political participation was so that it could serve as a means of strengthening President Syngman Rhee's political power base; paradoxically, the political system was highly centralized rather than decentralized by the introduction of local elections (Kim and Chung, 1995). Although decentralization is mostly regarded as a way to delegate power to lower levels, President Syngman Rhee utilized this method to ensure that local power bases were occupied by his political supporters.

In addition, there were mechanisms that enabled the central government's policy directives to be implemented without obstruction from local governments. For the provincial governments, the president of the Republic appointed the chief executives based on recommendations of the Minister of the Interior, who was one of his closest collaborators. This method of appointing leadership positions in the local governments made provincial government comply with the central government, so that central government policies did not encounter local governments' opposition. In addition, agencies and organizations delegated functions in a way that kept local governments under central governmental supervision, and local governments were strictly required to follow national-level policy directives in implementing the functions delegated to them by the central government (Kim, 2003; 328).

In 1960, the Second Republic was established after the first president, Syngman Rhee resigned from office. Efforts during the

Second Republic to make the government more decentralized were halted by the coup in 1961. Relations during this period can be regarded as following the Controlled Decentralization Model, in which the central government, using direct or indirect means, retained its power of control over local governments, even though those offices were filled by local elections.

The Korean economy in this period performed miserably due to the accumulation of effects stemming from previous historical periods when the Japanese colonial government from 1910 to 1945 had exploited the Korean economy for its own interest. The situation was then worsened by the Korean War from 1950 to 1953 which had ruined practically all infrastructure and social capital. Korea was one of the poorest countries in the world with one of the lowest economic growth rates in the world. The apparent decentralization of the political system did not contribute at all to the country's economic growth. All the mediating factors included in the framework of the current study were abysmal.

1962–1991: Deconcentration Model

During this period, economic development was highly emphasized. The efficient use of national resources and their mobilization was stressed by the central government. Local autonomy was suspended by a Special Law on Local Autonomy. Consequently all mayors and governors were appointed by the central government, and all appointed chief executives were expected to implement nationwide development plans and directives. In addition, the roles and functions of local councils were taken over by the central government. However, it can never be said that decentralized governance was totally stopped. Instead, administrative decentralization was carried out in order to efficiently execute the central government's development plan.

After the military coup in 1961, there was a military government whose reign was limited to two years. The reform agenda of this military government made up the basic elements of governance during this period and had lingering influences during the rest of President Park's regime, so it is worth looking closely at this government's policies. Many of the central government ministers and provincial governors were generals of the armed forces thus it serves as no surprise that the first Minister of the Interior was a general. He conducted an inspection tour of the provinces and upon completing his tour said that there was a lack of coordination and a lack of initiative on the part of local administrators (Cho, 1966). However, the minister was asked to delegate the authority of the central government to the local governments by a section chief of the Ministry of the Interior and by its bureau chief (ibid.). From this time, administrative decentralization began. According to Cho (1966; 24), the guidelines discussed in the first governor's meeting after the military coup were as follows:

> "The central government will have a planning function, the provincial government will have both planning and executing functions, and the cities and counties will have executing functions."

On 28 August 1961, General Park Chung Hee, the chairman of the Security Council of National Reform, said that the government would decentralize to a great extent and that the central government would only do the planning, coordination, and supervision, so the governments below the provincial level should have executing functions (Cho, 1966; 26).

On January 24, 1962, the chairman said that successful implementation of the five-year economic development plan was the most important goal; the Minister of Interior, on the other hand, said that strengthening the functions of local government was equally important (Cho, 1966). Cho has pointed out, however, that leaders of the military government applied their military education to civilian administration, and hence the concept of division between planning and execution was based on their military experience. With regard to interagency cooperation, the chairman said that if one is going to develop a basic plan for a field operation in the army, the planning for logistical support should go together with it (Cho, 1966; 37). This military analogy helped them to realize the need for delegation of authority, which would bring administrative efficiency (Cho, 1966).

This policy agenda of economic planning and administrative decentralization in order to efficiently execute their grand plan lasted throughout this period with some variations. But the Third Republic, inaugurated after the constitutional reform, stated that the local council election had to be postponed until the unification of the two Koreas. Let alone the Fourth Republic, the constitution of the Fifth Republic once again delayed local elections, stipulating that local councils should be established on an incremental basis taking into account the level of financial self-sufficiency attained by the localities.

The degree of decentralization during this period can be classified as following the Deconcentration Model, which refers to a system where local officials are appointed by the central government but exercise relatively strong decision-making power as the central government delegates its power to local agencies as well as local governments. Explaining decentralization in this period with the Deconcentration Model, however, does not mean that the central power over local government was weak in an absolute sense.

In fact, the central power in this period was strong enough to consistently pursue an export-driven economic development policy. Nonetheless, the reason for identifying this period as following the Deconcentration Model is that there was a delegation of governmental functions to local government and thus the central government did not do everything.

Korea experienced spectacular, usually double-digit, economic growth in this period. Mobilization of resources to focus on strategic areas of economic development was possible thanks to a strong bureaucracy based on the Deconcentration Model. The administrative capacity has played a great role in this process of extraordinarily high economic growth, while the other mediating variables have improved gradually.

1992–Present: Controlled Decentralization Model

As economic growth continued to increase subsistence levels, Korean society became increasingly diverse (Lee, 1995). The people, especially young people, aspired to western democratization, and in this sense, decentralization was regarded as one of the indicators of political democratization. From the early stage of the Sixth Republic, people started to request political decentralization of local governance.

In 1987, the ruling party proposed an amendment to the Local Autonomy Law; the seventh amendment of the Local Autonomy Act passed the National Assembly on 6 April 1988. The amendment stipulated that city and county councils were to be formed by 30 April, but permitted the executives of local governments to be appointed during the transition period. City and county council elections were held on March 26, 1991 and the provincial council elections on June 20, 1991. Thus, the Korean government has been politically decentralized, and the local governments' decision-making autonomy has steadily increased.

The Controlled Decentralization Model of this period does not mean that the central power was stronger than during the period from 1962 to 1991, which is identified as Deconcentration Model in this chapter. The reason for categorizing this period as Controlled Decentralization is that the power of the central government was still too strong to be characterized by the Decentralization Model. The period from 1948 to 1961 is also characterized by the Controlled Decentralization Model, but we cannot say the central power over local government after 1992 is as strong as that of the period 1948; local elections during the Syngman Rhee administration were conducted just in order to strengthen the president's political domination.

In spite of these relatively drastic reforms, the great power that the central government exercises over the local government has been gradually weakened, to the extent that the Ministry of the Interior, whose name is now Ministry of Home Affairs and Decentralization, employs various strategies to maintain its influence over local governments (Im, 2004). Park (2006) pointed out that the local government remained functionally and financially limited despite its constitutionally guaranteed autonomy for several reasons:

- The structure of local governance is largely fragmented and dispersed, and local decisions are subject to strong central control.
- Local electoral politics are increasingly nationalized, and the local chief executive does not share local governmental power with other local political actors.
- Economic interests and social identities at the local level are poorly organized and barely active. Local residents remain politically passive and hardly empowered.

- Principal actors in the local arena spent time developing new rules, so that many problems that local councilors as well as mayors and governors were involved in were discovered (Im, 2004).

Relationship between Decentralization and Economic Growth in Korea

It is often argued that the Korean government has functioned for many decades as an extremely centralized unitary system. This, however, does not necessarily mean that every decision in the Korean political system was made exclusively by the central government. In practice, the centralized system dispersed decision-making power to the various locations around the country to a great extent, as we have examined above.

The Korean experience of decentralization can be analyzed as Table 2 shows.

Table 2. Changes in the Model of Local Governance in Korea

1948–1961	1962–1991	1992–present
Controlled Decentralization (Apparent Decentralization)	Deconcentration	Controlled Decentralization

Figure 2. Korea's Annual GDP Growth Rate From 1961

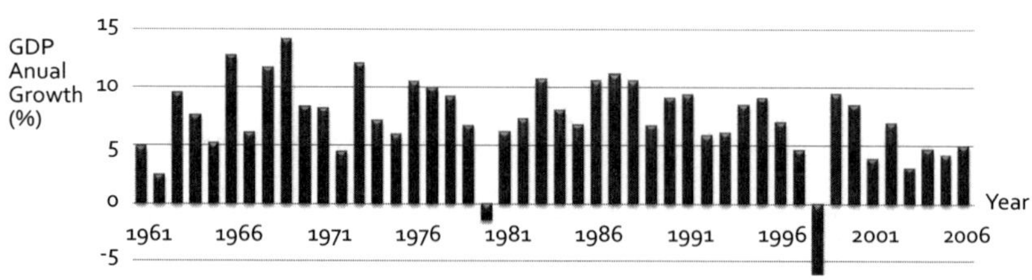

The annual GDP growth rate of Korea from 1961, presented in Figure 2, shows that Korea achieved a high level of economic development. Especially during the period from 1962 to 1991, when the average annual growth rate was more than 8 percent.

Unfortunately, there is little data available to clearly prove that Korea's Deconcentration Model during the developing period contributed directly or indirectly to this high level of economic growth. It is, however, not meaningless to try to explain the relationship, because the centralized governance system was one of Korea's defining features during this period.

In our theoretical prediction, summarized above in Table 2, the Deconcentration Model can prevent corruption, macroeconomic instability, and elite capture, and can foster high administrative capacity in local government. We can also say that the Korean government's choice of a centralized system that decentralized administrative authority, helped avoid the risks associated with decentralization to which developing countries are especially vulnerable. Thus economic development was not affected by these risks.

Although there are few materials to prove the relationship between the Deconcentration Model and the avoidance of risks related to decentralization, it is not impossible to explain it partially. For example, Cho (2004) insisted, based on the number of public servants punished by disciplinary action (see Figure 3), that local elections in Korea in the early 1990s were likely to produce more corrupt behaviors. It is argued that the number of disciplinary cases increased in the early 1990s when local elections took place. Furthermore, the numbers in the years 1990, 1993, and 1998 show high increases; there were local elections before or after these times.

Figure 3. Number of Public Servants Punished by Disciplinary Action

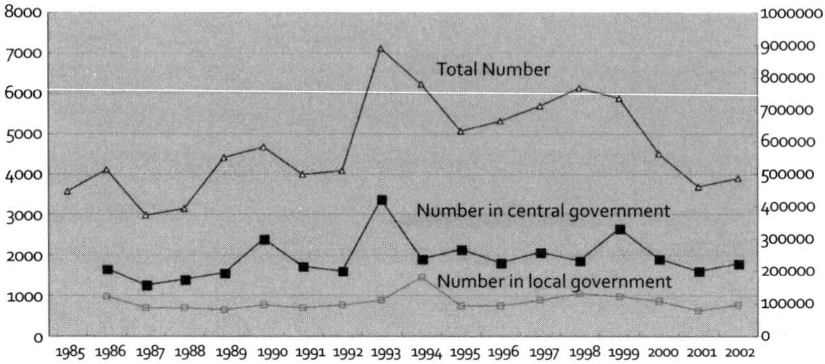

Notes: This graph has been adapted from Cho (2004).

Kim (2007) pointed out the low capacity of public servants in the Korean government during the 1960s. At that time, two-thirds of the mid-level public employees in central government were not educated at or beyond the high school level. They rarely received further education or long-term training after they became public servants, and salaries were very low. This lack of administrative capacity was an even more serious problem for local government. The president launched an initiative to make central government more effective by educating central government officials and dispatching them to local government instead of conducting local elections. It seems that this approach could potentially minimize the possible negative effects of low level of administrative capacity in local government.

It needs to be noted that the highly centralized government during the period from 1962 to 1991 partly devolved its administrative function to local government. Unlike the Centralization Model, this type of governance can, to some extent, exploit the benefits of the information advantage, which increases economic efficiency. These findings can support the theoretical predictions of this study, however, the supporting evidence is not sufficient, and further studies are needed to firmly establish this relationship.

Concluding Remarks

This study examines the effect of decentralization on a country's economic growth. Special focus has been placed upon the time dimension of the relationship between decentralization and growth. Decentralization can increase administrative capacity of a country from a certain period. If decentralization reforms are introduced earlier than this time period, it will make the decision-making system inefficient by distracting the system with many issues rather than focusing on the critical issue of the development of the country. In a practical sense, decentralization has a close relationship with the administrative capacity of a country.

In developing nations, a negative relationship was found between political decentralization and economic growth while there is not a statistically significant relationship between fiscal decentralization and economic growth. These results convey an important practical implication for those countries who have been trying to drastically decentralize their political system. If they pursue the economic growth as the policy priority, it is better not to hasten political decentralization. Contrary to the policy goal that the decentralization reform seeks, the country's economy will slow down or degrade due to the reform. It is in this context that developing nations need to study South Korea's case because the policies employed by the Korean Government resulted in faster paced economic growth due to the timely adoption of decentralization reforms. She had kept a centralized model during the rapid economic growth period and sacrificed a more immediate implantation of decentralization reforms. Once her economic level arrived at the semi-developed level, in mid 1990s precisely, political decentralization began being introduced.

In sum, decentralization is not a panacea for economic development for all categories of countries. To the contrary, it will operate as an obstacle to economic growth in certain conditions. A special caution needs to be taken regarding the time dimension before a developing country introduces political as well as fiscal decentralization reforms.

The Korean case is examined due to its implications for developing countries where decentralization is being promoted. Attention was concentrated on the indirect relationships in which several factors can play a role. Within our framework of analysis, we argued that the Deconcentration Model, as applied in Korea from 1960 to 1991, could help avoid the risks associated with decentralization to which developing countries are especially vulnerable, such as corruption and lack of administrative capacity in local government, and could also help keep economic development from being negatively affected by these risks.

Although Korea's successful economic growth can partly support this argument, there is not enough evidence to prove it, and further research is needed. Nonetheless, we can say that it is safer to start local governance when a country has the capability and the mature democracy to absorb the risks and problems that decentralization may bring about. Until a certain stage of progress is reached, a strong central government that decentralizes its executive functions can be beneficial. Simply copying and rapidly introducing western-style decentralization reforms is likely to harm economic growth and, in turn, to harm democracy in developing countries.

Note

The first half of this chapter was published in Im, T and W, Cho. 2008. Decentralization and Economic Growth in Korea, *Korean Journal of Policy Studies* 23(1): 49–71 and the latter part of this chapter was published in Im, T. 2010. Does Decentralization Reform Always Increase Economic Growth?: A Cross County Comparison of the Performance, *International Journal of Public Administration* 33: 508–20.

References

World Bank. 2000. *World Development Report 1999/2000*, New York: Oxford University Press.

Akai, N. and M., Sakata. 2002. Fiscal Decentralization Contributes to Economic Growth: Evidence from State-Level Cross Sectional Data for the United States, *Journal of Urban Economics* 52: 93–108.

Andres, J. and I., Hernando. 1997. Does Inflation Harm Economic Growth? Evidence for the OECD, NBER Working Paper No. W6062.

Arikan, G.G. 2004. Fiscal Decentralization: A Remedy for Corruption? *International Tax and Public Finance* 11(2): 175–95.

Bahl, R. and J., Linn. 1994. Fiscal Decentralization and Intergovernmental Transfers in Less Developed Countries, *Publius* 24(1): 1–19.

Banfield, E.C. 1979. Corruption as a Feature of Governmental Organization, In Ekpo, M. ed. *Bureaucratic Corruption in Sub-saharan Africa: Toward a Search for Causes and Consequences*, Washington, D.C.: University Press of America.

Bardhan, P. 2002. Decentralization of Governance and Development, *Journal of Economic Perspectives* 16(4): 185–205.

Bardhan, P. and D., Mookherjee. 1998. Expenditure Decentralization and the Delivery of Public Services in Developing Countries, Working Paper. Berkeley: University of California.

_______. 1999. Relative Capture of Local and Central Governments: An Essay in the Political Economy of Decentralization, Working Paper. Boston University.

_______. 2000. Capture and Governance at Local and National Levels, *American Economic Review* 90(2): 135–39.

_______. 2002. Corruption and Decentralization of Infrastructure in Developing Countries, Working Paper. Berkeley: University of California.

Bird, R.M. 1993. Threading the Fiscal Labyrinth: Some Issues in Fiscal Decentralization, *National Tax Journal* 46: 207–27.

Breton, A. 1996. *Competitive Governments: An Economic Theory of*

Politics and Public Finance, Cambridge: Cambridge University Press.

Brueckner, J.K. 2000. Fiscal Decentralization in Developing Countries: The Effects of Local Corruption and Tax Evasion, *Annals of Economics and Finance* 1(1): 1–18.

Cho, E. 2004. Decentralization and Corruption: An Empirical Study Focusing on the Environmental Pollution on Korea, *Korean Local Government Studies* 8(2): 201–22.

Cho, S. 1966. Administrative Decentralization: A Case Study in the South Korean Military Government, *Haengjong Nonchong* 4(1): 21–39.

Davoodi, H. and H., Zou. 1998. Fiscal Decentralization and Economic Growth: A Cross-Country Study, *Journal of Urban Economics* 43(2): 244–57.

Dillinger, W.R. 1997. Brazil's State Debt Crisis: Lessons Learned. Economic Notes 14. Country Department 1: Latin America and the Caribbean, Washington, D.C.: World Bank.

_______. and G.E., Perry. 1999. Macroeconomic Management in Decentralized Democracies: The Quest for Hard Budget Constraints in Latin America, *Development in Latin America and the Caribbean: Decentralization and Accountability of the Public Sector*, Washington, D.C.: World Bank.

Fisman, R. and R., Gatti. 2002. Decentralization and Corruption: Evidence Across Countries, *Journal of Public Economics* 83(3): 325–45.

Fjeldstad, O. 2001. Taxation, Coercion and Donors: Local Government Tax Enforcement in Tanzania, *The Journal of Modern African Studies* 39(2): 289–306.

Goldsmith, A.A. 1999. Slapping the Grasping Hand: Slapping the Grasping Hand: Correlates of Political Corruption in Emerging Markets, *American Journal of Economics and Sociology* 58(4): 865–83.

Hoffman, B. 1999. Macroeconomic Impact of Decentralization,In J., Litvack and J., Seddon. eds. *Decentralization Briefing Notes*, WBI Working Papers.

Huther, J. and A., Shah. 1998. Applying a Simple Measure of Good Governance to the Debate on Fiscal Decentralization, World Bank Policy Research Working Paper No. 1894. Washington, D.C.: World Bank.

Iimi, A. 2005. Decentralization and Economic Growth Revisited: An Empirical Note, *Journal of Urban Economics* 57(3): 449–61.

Im, T. 2004. *Action Theory for Local Organizations*, Seoul: Pakyoungsa.

_______. 2005. Intergovernmental Relations and Decision-Making: Conflicts and Cooperation in South Korea's Local Governments. In C., Ahn. ed. *New Development in Local Democracy and Decentralization in East Asia: Korea in Comparative Perspective*, Seoul: Seoul National University Press.

_______. (forthcoming), Does Decentralization Reform Always Increase Economic Growth? A Cross Country Comparison of the Perfomance, *International Journal of Public Administration.*

Jutting, J.P., C., Kauffman, I., McDonnell, H., Osterrieder, N., Pinaud, and L., Wegner 2004. Decentralisation and Poverty in Developing Countries: Exploring the Impact, OECD Development Centre Working Paper No. 236.

Kim, B. and C., Chung. eds. 1995. *Korea's Decentralization of 1950s*, Seoul: SNU Press.

Kim, C. 2007. *The Korean Presidents: Leadership for Nation Building*, Norwalk, CT: EastBridge.

Kim, S. 2003. A Comparative Study of Decentralization Reform between Japan and Korea, Paper presented at the 3rd International Conference of the Seoul Association for Public Administration (SAPA).

Lee, D. 1995. Politics of Decentralization: Changing Intergovernmental Relations in Korea, Paper presented at the KAPA International Symposium.

Lin, J.Y. and Z., Liu. 2000. Fiscal Decentralization and Economic Growth in China, *Economic Development and Cultural Change* 49(1): 1–21.

Litvack, J.I., J., Ahmad and R.M., Bird. 1998. *Rethinking Decentralization in Developing Countries*, Washington, D.C.: World Bank.

Ma, J. 1995. *Macroeconomic Management and Intergovernmental Relations in China*, World Bank Policy Research Working Paper No. 1408. Washington, D.C.: World Bank.

Mana, B. 1999. An Anti-Corruption Strategy for Provincial Government in Papua New Guinea, Asia Pacific School of Economics and Management, Working Papers. Canberra, Australia: Asia Pacific Press.

Mani, D. 2003. Human Security and Decentralized Planning: The Training Experience of UNCRD, Presented in the workshop on Decentralization and Poverty Reduction, Dakar, Senegal.

Martinez-Vazquez, J. and R.M., McNab. 2003. Fiscal Decentralization and Economic Growth, *World Development* 31(9): 1597–616.

Oates, W.E. 1972. *Fiscal Federalism*, New York: Harcourt Brace Jovanovich.

_______. 1993. Fiscal Decentralization and Economic Development, *National Tax Journal* 46(2): 237–43.

_______. 1999. An Essay on Fiscal Federalism, *Journal of Economic Literature* 37(3): 1120–49.

Oatley, T. 1999. Central Bank Independence and Inflation: Corporatism, Partisanship, and Alternative Indices of Central Bank Independence, *Public Choice* 98(3–4): 399–413.

Olowu, D. 2000. Bureaucracy and Democratic Reform, In G., Hyden, D., Olowu, Ogendo, W.O., Hastings and H.W.O. Okoth-Ogendo. eds. *African Perspectives of Governance*, Trenton/Asmara: Africa World Press.

Park, C. 2006. Local Governance and Community Power in Korea, *Korea Journal* 46(4): 9–32.

Prud'homme, R. 1995. The Dangers of Decentralization, *The World Bank Research Observer* 10(2): 201–20.

Rondinelli, D.A. and J.R., Nellis. 1986. Assessing Decentralization Policies in Developing Countries: The Case for Cautious Optimism, *Development Policy Review* 4: 3–23.

Rondinelli, D.A. 1999. What Is Decentralization? In Litvack, J. and Seddon, J. eds. *Decentralization Briefing Notes*, WBI Working Papers.

Seddon, J. 1999. Decentralization and Economic Growth, In Litvack, J. and Seddon, J. eds. *Decentralization Briefing Notes*. WBI Working Papers.

Shleifer, A. and R.W., Vishny. 1993. Corruption, *The Quarterly Journal of Economics* 108(3): 599–617.

Smoke, P. 1994. *Local Government Finance in Developing Countries: The Case of Kenya*, Nairobi: Oxford University Press.

Tanzi, V. 2000. Some Politically Incorrect Remarks on Decentralization and Public Finance, In J.J., Dethier. ed. *Governance, Decentralization and Reform in China, India and Russia*, Dordrecht: Kluwer Academic Publishers.

Thiessen, U. 2000. *Fiscal Federalism in Western European and Selected Other Countries: Centralization or Decentralization? What Is Better for Economic Growth?* DIW Discussion Paper No. 224. Berlin: DIW.

Tiebout, C.M. 1956. A Pure Theory of Local Expenditures, *Journal of Political Economy* 64(5): 416–24.

Treisman, D. 2000a. Decentralization and the Quality of Government (mimeo, Department of Political Science, University of California, Los Angeles).

_______. 2000b. The Causes of Corruption: A Cross National Study, *Journal of Public Economics* 76(3): 399–457.

Weingast, B.R. 1995. The Economic Role of Political Institutions: Market-Preserving Federalism and Economic Development, *Journal of Law, Economics and Organization* 11(1): 1–31.

Wunsch, J.S. and D., Olowu. 1990. *The Failure of the Centralized State: Institutions and Self Governance in Africa*, Boulder, Colorado: Westview Press.

Xie, D., H., Zou and H., Davoodi. 1999. Fiscal Decentralization and Economic Growth in the United States, *Journal of Urban Economics* 45(2): 228–39.

Zhang, T. and H., Zou. 1998. Fiscal Decentralization, Public Spending, and Economic Growth in China, *Journal of Public Economics* 67(2): 221–40.

Chapter 4 |

Changing Policy Orientation after Decentralization: Development or Welfare?

YUNHO KANG

Introduction

Local government heads (mayors), officials, and councilors (council members) cannot always be regarded as public-interest-seekers who try to only increase the benefits of citizens. They also seek to achieve their own self-interests, as proven by the fact that many mayors and councilors tend to be corrupt or despotic, and they are likely to focus on pork-barrel projects in order to be reelected in Korea.

What strategies then, do they use for their own self-interests? What policies do mayors and councilors as politicians prefer and carry out in order to be reelected? What policies do local government officials give priority to in order to attain individual benefits such as budget increases and career advancement?

Regarding these issues, two conflicting arguments exist. Some analysts argue that local governments give priority to policies related to regional development (Peterson, 1981; Kernell, 1986;

Hibbs, 1987; Heidenheimer et al., 1983; Schneider, 1989). Others conclude that local governments give preference to policies on social welfare (Wildavsky, 1974; Rourke, 1984; Wong, 1988).

In Korea, after the decentralization reform, researchers analyzed what effects decentralization had on social welfare policies in local governments. The results varied according to the research objects, analysis periods, and methodologies (Ryu, 1999; Gang, 2000; Lee, 2001; Kim, 2001).

These preceding studies analyzed the effects of decentralization on the respective areas of policy, focusing on social welfare policy. However, they did not analyze the relative relationship between the areas of policy. That is, the analyses did not deal with how local governments prioritized respective policy areas, and what factors contribute to the differences in relative priority on areas of policy. Therefore, it is very important to identify those policies which local governments have prioritized and determine what factors caused those policy preferences, after the implementation of local autonomy. This kind of analysis will provide information necessary for predicting the direction of local governmental policies and control the policies so that they move in a socially useful direction.

Under these research questions, this chapter purposes to classify local governments' policy orientations into a few types and analyze the attributes of the policy orientations caused by the decentralization. Then, the chapter will identify the causes which produce the differences of the policy orientations among local governments. From this analysis, implications can be inferred that help to: identify the direction and characteristics of local governments' policy orientations, predict the direction of the policy, and control the policy in a socially beneficial and responsible direction.

Literature Review

The theory on policy orientation of local government may be divided into two parts: 1) a development-oriented theory (an economic perspective) and 2) a welfare-oriented theory (a political perspective). The former says that politicians or policy-makers in local government will seek to achieve regional economic growth and, thus, give higher priority to regional development policy than social welfare policy. Welfare-oriented theory, on the other hand, concludes that the major goal of politicians or policy-makers is to reinforce social welfare policy, because this allows them to gain political support for future reelection.

According to the political perspective, policy makers of local governments actively carry out social welfare policy to gain political support from local residents. In other words, under the political perspective, a local government cannot—and will not—pay extensive attention to regional development policy which is advantageous to regional economic growth at the expense of social welfare policy which is not advantageous to the economic growth. If a local government thinks it is politically rational, though economically irrational, to give priority to social welfare policy, that government will be oriented towards social welfare policy (Wildavsky, 1974; Rourke, 1984; Wong, 1988).

On the contrary, according to the economic perspective, policy-makers of local governments focus on regional development policy to facilitate regional economic growth. This is because, without economic growth in the region, the mobilization of finances necessary to operate local government is difficult, and economic growth is the most reliable policy alternative to insure the public support.

Another reason policy-makers focus on regional economic growth is that the bankruptcy of regional commerce, an increase in unemployment, the fall of land prices, and failure of other economic indicators due to slowdown of economic growth can be fatal to local governments' politicians and officials as well as citizens (Peterson, 1981; Kernell, 1986; Hibbs, 1987).

Additionally, local government cannot achieve political support by the use of social welfare policy, in that the benefits of social welfare policy are restricted to only a small segment of local residents, while the benefits of regional development policy can be realized by virtually all regional residents. Thus, local government prefers to implement regional development policy to improve economic growth and avoids social welfare policy which tends to stunt growth (Peterson, 1981; Heidenheimer et al., 1983; King, 1984; Schneider, 1989).

Peterson (1981) suggests the "hypothesis of city limits" which argues that city governments which compete to procure productive resources—under the constraints of regional economic structures in which labor and capital freely move in and out—are limited rather than free in their choice of policies. That is, city governments cannot help but to seek development policies which are favorable to inviting labor and capital resources, and avoiding social welfare policies which are obstacles to inviting them. Thus, city governments become development-oriented, while avoiding redistribution policies.

On the other hand, the direction of local governmental policies can be inferred from classic studies of American democracy. Schattschneider (1960: 4–16) concludes that the narrower the scale of political conflict, the greater the tendency that policies, which are favorable to organized interests, or conservative forces, are adopted. Thus, in a local government whose scale of political conflict is narrower than that of a central government, the tendency is strong to facilitate and further the benefits of the privileged in the region, such as large-scale companies or land owners.

There are empirical studies which analyzed policy orientations of local governments. Wilensky (1981), Cameron (1978), and DeViney (1983), et al. performed cross-sectional analyses of policy orientations of local governments in America and European countries. The results are similar: the higher the degree of decentralization, the less the expenditures by the local government on social welfare. These results support the economic perspective.

In Korea, these kinds of analyses have focused on the effects of implementation of local autonomy on social welfare policy. Only Ryu's analysis (1991) includes development policy, as well as social welfare policy. The results vary according to research object, analysis period, or analytic methodology. Thus, the results sometimes conflict each other (Lee and Kim, 1992; Ryu, 1999; Gang, 2000; Lee, 2001; Kim, 2001).

From a different perspective, Sellers and Lidstroem (2007: 609–632) demonstrated a close relationship between decentralization of local government and the character of the welfare state itself, focusing on Social Democratic welfare states. Local empowerment and the consequent strong local government helped make the construction of the Social Democratic welfare state possible for two reasons: 1) the resulting infrastructure gave local governments the administrative, legal, and fiscal capacities to pursue the universalistic, egalitarian aspirations of this welfare state and 2) the empowered local government provided a vehicle to mobilize local support for the welfare state.

These preceding analyses analyzed each policy area independently, largely focusing on social welfare policy but did not deal with relative priorities between respective policy areas.

This study presupposes that the effects of decentralization on the policies of local government vary according to each individual government. Thus, this study categorizes local governments based upon their respective policy orientation after decentralization. As for the analysis of policy orientation, the preceding theories and studies dealt with the policy areas separately. However, this study analyzes policy orientation from the perspective of the relationship between regional development and social welfare policy. That is, from this perspective, this study divides policy orientations of local governments into several categories: development-oriented, welfare-oriented, dually (development and welfare)-oriented, and dually-avoided. Then, this study finds the causes which produce differences in the policy orientation types among local governments. What policy areas receive priority from local government after decentralization, and why? This study, which seeks to answer these questions, can provide important information which is useful for predicting the direction of local governmental policies and controlling their direction toward socially desirable ends.

Methodology and Explanatory Model

Methodology

In Korea, the administrative structure of local autonomy is a two-tier system which consists of an upper-tier and lower-tier local government. All local governments have the same political regime which is similar to the presidential system that has separate executive and legislative bodies. These two bodies are composed of members who are directly elected by local residents. The chief officer of the executive body becomes the representative of the local government, or the mayor. All local governments have "strong mayor-weak council regimes," which grant the mayor (chief executive) stronger political powers than those granted to the council (the legislative body).

The period which is analyzed by this chapter ranges from 1993 to 1998, and includes three years before and three years after the initiation of popular election of mayors in June, 1995. The first research question of this study is: in the first term of popularly elected mayors (July 1995–June 1998), how did the local policy orientation change? And the second research question is: why did the change occur?

In Korea, it is generally believed that real decentralization started with the resumption of popularly electing of mayors in June, 1995. This is because, after this election, the mayor's status changed from national public servant (i.e., appointed by the president) to regional representative (i.e., elected by local residents) and, at the same time, his power also increased enough for him to be called "the small president of the region." Consequently with the change of the mayor's status, the mayor's goals might also change. The mayor, as a national public servant, tried to achieve job stability and was fiercely loyal to his appointer, the president. However, the mayor, as the residents' representative, seeks to maximize residents' support and secure votes in the following election. This change in the mayor's motivation might result in changes to the policy orientation of local government. Thus, it seems to be appropriate to provide a comparative analysis of policy orientation before and after the election in 1995.

Upper-tier local governments included seven metropolitan cities and nine provinces, and lower-tier local governments numbered 71 cities, 94 counties, and 69 districts (autonomous districts) in 1998. This chapter focuses on lower-tier local governments and analyzes 170 lower-tier local governments (33 cities, 90 counties, 47 districts) with merged or divided local governments during the analytical period excluded from the analysis.

Policy orientation will be classified as being focused on regional development and social welfare policy.

Budgets are a type of policy output. In this chapter, the measurement and classification of policy orientations of local governments will be implemented by analyzing the budgets of local governments. Factors affecting the policy orientation will be selected from the related preceding studies. The attributes of policy orientation after decentralization will be analyzed by both a Chi-Square Test and ANOVA (Analysis of Variance). The causal relationship between policy orientation and factors affecting it will be tested by Logistic Regression.

Explanatory Model

The Logistic Regression Model, which will be used for the analysis of the causal relationship mentioned above, is as follows:

Policy Orientation = *f* (Local fiscal capacity,
Urbanization rate,
Degree of residential support for mayor,
Degree of residential support for councilor,
Mayor's registered party (ruling party),
Mayor's registered party (nonpartisan),
Mayor's educational background,
Councilor's educational background,

Mayor's public career,
Councilor's public career,
Councilor's political career.

Dependent Variable

In this analysis, the policy orientation of local government is a dependent variable. In the popularly elected mayors' first term (July 1995–June 1998), whether the policy of local government became development-oriented or welfare-oriented when compared to the previous administration will be analyzed. Then, the results of the analysis will be classified into several types. The analysis will be performed based on the budget of local government. The policy orientation will be classified based on both regional economic development expenditures and social security expenditures. That is, the classification will be performed based on the change in respective area expenditures (budgets) between the three years of the popularly elected mayors' first term and the prior three years (between the three year periods of FYs 1996–98 and the three year periods of FYs 1993–95).

As shown in Table 1, nine policy orientations are logically possible. The ratio of 1) regional economic development expenditure and 2) social security expenditure to the total expenditure has three types of change after the election (decentralization), respectively: 1) increase, 2) no change, and 3) decrease. Thus, when the policies are combined according to the three types of change each could have, there are nine possible orientations ($3 \times 3 = 9$).

In Table 1, policy orientation types (1) include four types: 1) development-oriented, 2) welfare-oriented, 3) dually (development and welfare)-oriented, and 4) dually-avoided. This indicator will be used to analyze policy orientation attributes of local government, which are analyzed by both Chi-Square Test and ANOVA.

Policy orientation types (2) will be used to analyze factors which produce the differences in policy orientation among local governments. This analysis is performed by logistic regression. In order to find why the local government is development—or welfare-oriented, two (development-oriented and welfare-oriented) of the four types of policy orientations will be analyzed, because, whether the local government seeks development policy or welfare policy is evident in these two types, while it is not evident in the other two (both-oriented and both-avoided). Development-oriented and welfare-oriented are coded "0" and "1," respectively (see Table 1).

Table l. The Policy Orientation Types of the Local Government

Serial No.	Change of development exp.[a]	Change of social security exp.[b]	Policy orientation types (1)	Policy orientation types (2)
1	Increase	Increase	Both-oriented	Excluded[d]
2	Increase	No change	No case[c]	No case
3	Increase	Decrease	Development-oriented	Development-Oriented (= 0)
4	No change	Increase	No case	No case
5	No change	No change	No case	No case
6	No change	Decrease	No case	No case
7	Decrease	Increase	Welfare-oriented	Welfare-oriented (=1)
8	Decrease	No change	No case	No case
9	Decrease	Decrease	Both-avoided	Excluded

a. The increase or decrease of the development expenditure ratio after decentralization when compared to before decentralization.
b. The increase or decrease of the ratio of social security expenditure after decentralization when compared to before decentralization.
c. No local government is included in these types, since "no change" is not found in the budget.
d. Excluded from the analysis.

Independent Variables

The independent variables and their indicators for the analysis of determinants of policy orientation are shown in Table 2. As for socioeconomic factors, local fiscal capacity reflects the "hypothesis of financial constraints" where welfare expenditures of local government are proportionate to the fiscal capacity of the government (Peterson, 1981; Chamlin, 1987; So and Kim, 1999). The urbanization rate reflects the point of view that, according to the degree of urbanization in the local government, the demand for regional policies and the resulting policy orientations of regional policymakers will vary (Clark and Ferguson, 1983; Chung, 1988; Gang, 2001). In practice, these socioeconomic factors may be proxies for the type of local government, in that in Korea, the type of local government is classified mainly according to environmental criteria (especially population), not institutional criteria. Political factors are selected in order to reflect that process and contents of policy are affected by the degree of residents' support for regional politicians, the politicians' registered parties, etc. (So, 1996: 174–175; Lim, 1999). Individual factors reflect the point of view that the process and contents of policy vary according to politicians' expertise or public career, etc. (So, 1996: 174–175; Lim, 1999).

Table 2. Independent Variables and Their Indicators

Factors	Variables	Indicators	Remarks
Socio-economic	Local fiscal capacity	Degree of local finance independence (%)	Average (1996–97)
	Urbanization rate	Local government's population density (person)	
Political	Residential support degree for mayor	Mayor's rate of vote-obtaining (%)	June/1995 Local election
	Residential support degree for councilor	Councilors' average rate of votes obtained (%)	
	Mayor's registered party: ruling party	Ruling party=1, opposition party and nonpartisan=0	
	Mayor's registered party	Nonpartisan=1, ruling and opposition party=0	
Individual	Mayor's educational background	Mayor's years of being in school (year)	June/1995 Local election
	Councilor's educational background	Councilors' average years of being in school (year)	
	Mayor's public career	Does=1, does not=0	
	Councilor's public career	Rate of councilors in possession of public career (%)	
	Councilor's political	Rate of reelected councilors (%)	

Sources: Data about socioeconomic factors are from *Major Statistic Indicators in City, County, and District* (Korea National Statistical Office, 1999). Data about both political and individual factors are from *1st Comprehensive Book of Whole Local Election* (National Election Commission, 1995).

a. In the local election in 1995, party nomination of candidates is allowed only for mayors, not councilors by law.
b. As for the local election in 1995, it is the 1st for mayors, but the 2nd for councilors, so a portion of them were reelected.
c. For the local governments which had a midterm election during the 1st half of a popularly elected mayors' first term, the data from the midterm election were used. This is because the term of those who were elected at the midterm election were longer than those who were elected in the prior election.
d. The ratio of its own revenue (excluding grants and subsidies from the central government) to total budget in a local government ((local tax + other revenue except local tax) / total budget * 100).

Research Findings

Policy Orientation: Development or Welfare?

In order to identify the characteristics of local governments' policy orientation, a Chi-square test was performed between policy orientation types (1) in Table 1 and local government types (city, county, and district) (see Table 3). The results show that the policy orientations of local government vary according to the types of local government. Of the total 170 cases (local governments), dually (development and welfare)-oriented represented the highest number of cases at 83 (48.8%). The number of development-oriented cases was 42 (24.7%), while welfare-oriented cases were 37 (21.8%). Dually (development and welfare)-avoided cases were came in the lowest at 8 (4.7%).

Let's now turn to the distribution of frequency according to the type of local government. Among the 33 cities in this research, 22 (66.7%) were dually-oriented and 9 (27.3%) were development-oriented. The number of welfare-oriented and dually-avoided was very scarce, with 1 case (3.3%) each. In the category of counties, 90 cases were researched, and of these, 42 cases (46.7%) were dually-oriented and 31 cases (34.4%) were development-oriented. Welfare-oriented and dually-avoided had a small distribution of 10 cases (11.1%) and 7 cases (7.8%), respectively. Districts showed a very different distribution from cities and counties. Of the total 47 districts, welfare-oriented districts were identified in as many as 26 cases (55.3%), and dually-oriented were identified in 19 cases (40.4%). Development-oriented consisted of only 2 cases (4.3%). Dually-avoided cases were not found.

Let us look at the distribution according to the type of policy orientation. Of the 42 cases in development-oriented, so many 31

(73.8%) were distributed in counties, 9 (21.4%) were distributed in cities, and only 2 (4.8%) were distributed among districts. On the other hand, of the 37 cases in the welfare-oriented category, as many as 26 cases (70.3%) were distributed in districts, and only 1 (2.7%) and 10 cases (27.0%) were distributed in cities and counties, respectively. Dually-oriented and dually-avoided were found more often in counties than in cities or districts.

The results of a Chi-square test show that there is a significant relationship between local governmental type and policy orientation type at the significance level of 0.01. That is, the distribution of policy orientation type is significantly different between local governmental types. Cities (as small—or middle—cities) and counties (located in rural areas) may be development-oriented, in that most of them are undeveloped or developing areas and, thus, are faced with increasing demands for development. Also, their development functions or affairs are relatively larger than those of districts. Unlike cities and counties, districts (located in metropolitan cities) may be relatively welfare-oriented, in that they are much more developed already and thus, they are faced with more welfare demands than developmental demands. Additionally, their own developmental functions or affairs are smaller than those of cities and counties.

Resulting from the fact that about one-half of local governments (48.8%) were dually-oriented indicates that both development and welfare policy are relatively important to regional residents when compared to other policy areas. As a result, many governments have sought to reinforce both policy areas, if they could. City governments were more oriented to dually-oriented when compared to counties and districts. Cities have a higher fiscal capacity and consequently a higher level of autonomy and policy ability than the other two. So, perhaps, many cities (66.7%) could reinforce both of them.

On the other hand, dually-avoided cases were very scarce. This implies that avoiding the two policy areas all-together is difficult for local governments. Although the two policy areas are both very important, a few governments weakened both policies. Most of the dually-avoided cases (87.5%) were distributed among counties. Counties have very small populations and low fiscal capacity, so the resulting policy autonomy is also very low. Under these situations, some county governments hardly mobilize finances even for current expenses, and do not have enough of a margin to imple-

Table 3. Policy Orientation Distribution According to Local Governmental Types (Policy Orientation *Local Governmental type Crosstab)

			Policy orientation (1)				Total
			D'vlpment-oriented	Welfare-oriented	Both – oriented	Both-avoided	
Govt type	City	Count	9	1	22	1	33
		% within govt	27.3	3.0	66.7	3.0	100.0
		% within orient'n	21.4	2.7	26.5	12.5	19.4
		% total	5.3	0.6	12.9	0.6	19.4
	Cnty	Count	31	10	42	7	90
		% within govt	34.4	11.1	46.7	7.8	100.0
		% within orient'n	73.8	27.0	50.6	87.5	52.9
		% total	18.2	5.9	24.7	4.1	52.9
	Dist	Count	2	26	19	0	47
		% within govt	4.3	55.3	40.4	0.0	100.0
		% within orient'n	4.8	70.3	22.9	0.0	27.6
		% total	1.2	15.3	11.2	0.0	27.6
	Tot	Count	42	37	83	8	170
		%within govt	24.7	21.8	48.8	4.7	100.0
		%within orient'n	100.0	100.0	100.0	100.0	100.0
		%total	24.7	21.8	48.8	4.7	100.0

Pearson Chi-Square Value=52.957, df=6, Asymp. Sig.(2-sided)=0.000

ment investment programs. Thus, for the governments who are dually-avoided, it seems that the dually-avoided policy orientation might be unavoidable.

Meanwhile, it also helps to identify the attributes of policy orientation in order to look at changes in the ratios of each area's budget after decentralization. ANOVA was performed on the 170 local governments in order to identify the changes according to local governmental types (see Table 4). After decentralization, the ratios of both development and welfare budgets increased, respectively. In total, the ratio of regional economic development expenditures increased much more than those of social security expenditures. The increasing rates varied according to local governmental types.

After decentralization, in total, the ratio of regional economic development expenditures increased by 111.8 percent. The increase in the ratio was highest in counties (152.0%), and smallest in districts (38.8%). The increasing rate of the ratio in cities was 106.3 percent. The average of change in the ratio of regional economic development expenditures was significantly different between local governmental types at the significance level of 0.01. In the case of social security expenditures, in total the ratio to total budget increased by 20.7 percent after decentralization. The increasing rates in cities and districts were similar, 37.9 percent and 37.5 percent, respectively. The increasing rate was smallest in counties (5.6%). The average value of change in the ratio of social security expenditures was also significantly different between local governmental types at the significance level of 0.01. These findings are consistent with the inferences mentioned above which state that the more urbanized an area of local government is, the higher priority that government places on social welfare policy, and the more rural an area of local government is, the higher priority that government places on regional development policy.

Even though the policy orientation of local governments was explained above according to the types of local governments, it was only to help understand the orientation. One of the core propositions in this chapter is that policy orientation will vary according to the situations or attributes of the government, regardless of local governmental types.

Table 4. Rate of Changes in Each Budget Ratio According to Local Governmental Type

	Govt Type	Number of case	Average	Standard deviation	F
Changing rate of regional economic development expenditure ratio	City	33	106.3	116.6	5.22
	County	90	152.0	219.0	
	District	47	38.8	188.3	
	Total	170	111.8	199.6	
Changing rate of social security expenditure ratio	City	33	37.9	69.0	15.97
	County	90	5.6	22.8	
	District	47	37.5	25.1	
	Total	170	20.7	40.0	

* $p < 0.01$

Why Development or Welfare?

In order to find a causal relationship between policy orientation types (2) in Table 1 (dependent variable) and socioeconomic/political/individual characteristic factors (independent variables), a logistic regression was performed. The results are shown in Table 5. First, let us see how appropriate the fit of the regression model is. In the model, value is 62.820 and the significance probability is 0.000 ($<\alpha=0.01$), so the model is statistically significant. In the Hosmer and Lemeshow Goodness-of-Fit Test, significance probability is 0.894 ($>\alpha=0.05$), so the model fits the data well. The percent correct of the model is also high (83.5%), so the model fits the data well.

Let us see the impact of each independent variable on the dependent variable. Diverse factors, such as socioeconomic, political, and individual factors, significantly affected the policy orientation (development—or welfare-oriented) of local governments.

In socioeconomic factors, both local fiscal capacity and urbanization rate of local government had a significant impact on the policy orientation of the government. The higher fiscal capacity the government had the more development-oriented and welfare-avoiding its policies were. This result is in conflict with the "hypothesis of financial constraints," defined by Chamlin (1987) in that welfare expenditures of local government are proportionate to the fiscal capacity of the government, while it is consistent with the conclusion by Cameron (1987) because the local government with a high fiscal capacity can meet social welfare demands with a relatively smaller ratio of budgets due to the fact that the higher a local government's fiscal capacity is, the lower its ratio of welfare expenditure is. Also, according to the result of this regression, the higher the urbanization rate of local government was, the more welfare-oriented and development-averse its policies were. This result is consistent with that of research done by Gang (2001) since the more urbanized the region, the greater the welfare demands are when compare to the development demands, and thus the local government will give higher priority to welfare policy. This result is also consistent with that of Table 3, analyzed above.

For political factors, the degree of residential support for both mayors and councilors was significantly related to the policy orientation of local government. The higher the residential support, the more a mayor and councilor prioritized welfare policies over development policies. This seems to indicate that the political ideologies of regional politicians placed greater importance on social welfare than development. According to the perspective of public choice theory which asserts that a politician's goal is to be reelected by obtaining political support—if a politician is supposed to be reelected without pursuing vote-maximizing policies due to weak competition among political parties—the politician will seek his ideal policies although they are not popular (Frey, 1978). Taking this point of view, regional politicians who have high residential support will pursue their ideal policies without being constrained by reelection concerns. Then, according to this study, the regional politicians who have high political support from regional residents gave priority to welfare policies. Thus, it seems that the political ideology of local politicians is skewed toward social welfare rather than development.

Among the individual characteristics of both mayors and councilors, only the mayor's educational background had significant impact on the dependent variable. The longer a mayor was in school, the more development-oriented and welfare-avoided his policies were. By logistic regression, it is difficult to identify the relative impact of independent variables upon the dependent variable. Partial correlation coefficients between dependent and independent variables are shown in Table 5. Based on the size of the coefficients, the order of the impacts of independent variables on the dependent variable is as follows (descending order): urbanization rate, local fiscal capacity, degree of residential support for councilor, degree of residential support for mayor, etc. However, it has limits when it comes to judging the relative impact of independent variables on the dependent variable based on the partial correlation coefficients.

Table 5. Logistic Regression Result of Determinants of Policy Orientation

	Regression coefficient	Wald	Correlation coefficient
Local fiscal capacity	−0.08	4.015	−0.136
Urbanization rate	0.00	6.231	0.197
Degree of residential support for mayor	0.	3.642	0.123
Degree of residential support for councilor	0.	3.913	0.132
Mayor-registered party (ruling party)	0.735	0.371	0.000
Mayor-registered party (nonpartisan)	0.748	0.469	0.000
Mayor's educational background	−0.	2.860	−0.089
Councilor's educational background	0.634	2.455	0.065
Mayor's public career	0.491	0.321	0.000
Councilor's public career	−0.056	2.044	−0.020
Councilor's political career	0.027	1.000	0.000
Constant	−14.05	3.987	
Model	=62.820 df=11 Sig.=0.000		
Hosmer and Lemeshow test	=3.572 df=8 Sig.=0.894		
Percent correct	83.5%		

* $p < 0.1$, ** $p < 0.05$

Implications and Conclusion

Results of this analysis showed that the policy orientation of local governments varied according to the situations or attributes of the governments. Furthermore, the results indicated that the factors affecting the diversity of the policy orientation are also diverse.

Policy orientation of local government reveals the following conclusions. After decentralization, both regional development and social welfare policies were mainly reinforced, although changes in orientation of development and welfare policies were different between local governments. As for the changes in relative priority between the two policy areas, development policy was slightly more reinforced than welfare policy. Cities, which have relatively high fiscal capacity and consequently a high degree of autonomy, were relatively more frequent in the dually-oriented type than counties and districts. The dually-avoided type, although it was very scarce, was mainly distributed in counties which have relatively low fiscal capacity and low autonomy. Districts, which are all located in metropolitan cities, were the most frequent practitioners of the welfare-oriented type.

Policy orientation of local government was affected by diverse factors such as socioeconomic, political, and local politicians' individual factors. Based on the respective impacts of both political and individual factors on the dependent variable, mayor-related variables were more commonly related with the policy orientation of local government than councilor-related variables. In other words, whether a local government is oriented towards development or welfare policies was more often affected by a mayor's characteristics or related variables rather than a councilor's characteristics or related variables.

This analysis provides the following implications with regard to decentralization. First, the results of the analysis of factors affecting local government's policy orientation help to predict the policy directions of the government. From the results, it can be conjectured that the local government which has high fiscal capacity, and whose mayor has a good educational background, will, afterwards, probably be more oriented towards regional development than social welfare. On the other hand, the local government which is located in an urban area, and whose politicians have obtained high political support from the residents, will probably give higher priority to welfare than development policy.

Second, the fact that policy orientation of local government is not single, but consists of diverse types such as development-oriented, welfare-oriented, dually-oriented, and dually-avoided, implies that, from now on, the measures to manage and control these policies in beneficial ways should also be diverse, rather than uniform. That is, measures to control policies should be different among development-oriented, welfare-oriented, dually-oriented, and dually-avoided local governments. For example, with the local government which is in trouble due to its politicians' excessive welfare orientation and development avoidance, balance between the two policy areas can be achieved by residents' withdrawing their political support for local politicians.

It is due to the results of this analysis that the local politicians who received high political support from regional residents gave policy priority to the welfare area. Besides, in this kind of local government atmosphere, in local elections, electing a mayor who has a good educational background can also be a measure of attaining balance between welfare and development policies. This inference also stems from the result of this analysis which demonstrates that a mayor with a good educational background was more oriented towards development than welfare policy.

Third, the finding that relative policy priority between regional development and social welfare areas was affected more by mayor-related variables than councilor-related variables indicates that a mayor's power or authority was stronger than the councilors'. Thus, institutional measures should be created which reinforce councilors' powers to create a check and balance system between a mayor and the councilors, in order to make the greatest use of the two institutions' opposing systems.

Fourth, being that both development and social welfare are essential for humans, it is necessary to give local governments more fiscal capacity and autonomy through financial decentralization. This is because city governments which had higher fiscal capacity and higher autonomy were more oriented towards reinforcing both areas of policies than any other types of local governments, while counties which had lower fiscal capacity and lower autonomy accounted for most of the dually-avoided policy orientations.

Note

The Korean version of this study has been published by Kang, Y. 2002. Policy Preferences and their Determinants in Korean Local Governments, *Korean Public Administration Review* 36(4): 227–41.

References

Cameron, D. 1978. The Expansion of Public Economy: A Comparative Analysis, *American Political Science Review* 72.

Chamlin, M.B. 1987. General Assistance among Cities: An Explanation of the Need, Economic Threat, and Benign Neglect Hypothesis, *Social Science Quarterly* 68: 834–46.

Clark, T.N. and L.C., Ferguson. 1983. City Money-Political Processes, Fiscal Strain, and Retrenchment, Columbia University Press.

DeViney, S. 1983. The Characteristic of the States and the Expansion of Public Social Expenditures, *Comparative Social Research* 6.

Frey, B.S. 1978. Modern Political Economy, New York: Wiley.

Heidenheimer, A., H., Helco and C., Adams. 1983. Comparative Public Policy: The Politics of Social Choice in Europe and America, New York: Martin's Press.

Hibbs, D. 1987. The American Political Economy: Macro-economics and Electorical Politics in the United States, Cambridge: Havard University Press.

Kernell, S. 1986. Going Public, *Congressional Quarterly* Washington.

Madison, J. 1961. No. 10, In H., Alexander, M., James and J., John, *The Federalist Papers,* New York: North American Library.

Peterson, P. 1981. City Limits, Chicago: University of Chicago Press.

Rourke, F.F. 1984. Bureaucracy, Politics, and Public Policy, 3rd ed. Boston: Little, Brown.

Schattschneider, E.E. 1960. Semi-Sovereign People, New York: Holt, Rinehart, & Winston.

Schneider, M. 1989. The Competitive City: The Political Economy of Suburbia, Pittsburgh: University of Pittsburgh Press.

Wildavsky. A. 1974. The Politics of Budgetary Process, 2nd ed. Boston: Little, Brown.

Wilensky, H. 1981. The New Corporatism, Centralization, and the Welfare State, Beverly Hills: Sage Publication.

Wong, K. 1988. Economic Constraint and Political Choice in Urban Policymaking, *American Journal of Political Science* 32.

Chapter 5 |

Morals or Money?: The Developmental Effects of the Casino Industry

SEONG RAK CHOI

Introduction

Some 2,000 casinos are currently in operation in a little over 120 countries around the world. This number has been rising, especially since 2004, which was the year in which the casinos in Macau turned out to be a great success. East Asia has seen a rapid proliferation of casinos: two casino complexes are being built in Singapore, where moral values have been held in high regard, and the establishment of casinos is also being considered in Japan and Thailand. As more people embrace the idea that building casinos can serve as a Midas touch in order to improve local growth, more efforts are being made in Asian countries to legalize gambling and build more casinos.

Originally, casinos were a social club where people gathered to socialize. However, there are other cases where casinos were built as a means of stimulating local development. This is particularly the case in East Asia, where most cases of building casinos represent not just simple businesses but rather a means of promoting the local economy. However, can the success of casinos really ensure local development? The success of a casino creates a lot of revenue and profit. An increase in profits in any industry, of course, creates greater tax revenues for the government. Can the success of casinos, however, be viewed as a true advancement when it comes to the development of a country? A number of discussions introducing the success of casinos often tell us how much profits casino operators earn, and how much of a contribution it made to the public purse. When policy makers however, permit the development of casinos in the first place, they are likely more concerned with the area's growth than casino profitability.

In Korea, Kangwon Land Casino was built to promote the local development of the Jeongseon area in Gangwon province, located on east coast of an economically underdeveloped region. In principle, Casinos are banned in Korea. The casinos which exist are restrictive and only allow foreign visitors. However Kangwon Land Casino is an exception and admits Korean citizens. The Korea Government licensed the casino and made it accessible to Koreans in order to stimulate the local economy.

A number of studies have found, since the opening of Kangwon Land Casino, that it has had a positive impact on the local economy. These studies, however, focus solely on the entrepreneurial success of Kangwon Land Casino. The establishment of Kangwon Land Casino, however, was not intended to successfully operate and make money, but to promote the development of the area. Accordingly, this study aims to review whether the establishment of Kangwon Land Casino has had a substantial impact on local development, primarily in terms of the local development indices often used in Korea. Given a growing chorus of voices in favor of the establishment of casinos as a policy choice which encourages high profits, a verification of whether their establishment might have a substantial impact on local development should be valuable.

Casinos and Local Development

Traditional Discussion

The casino, in a traditional context, served as a venue of socialization in European aristocracies of the 17th and 18th centuries. As more Europeans made it to other parts of the world in the 19th century, members-only casinos proliferated globally. These casinos served as places of socialization and sport; hence no discussion of the relationship between casinos and local development took place. In other words, casinos had barely anything to do with local development in their early stages.

It was due to the pro-casino policy of Las Vegas, Nevada, which dates back to the 1930s, which opened the public's eyes to casino's potential for local development. In order to promote local development and thereby help overcome the Great Depression, commercial type casinos were developed in Nevada. The success of this pro-casino policy has made the Las Vegas of today the gambling Mecca of the world. The success of Las Vegas casinos, however, was somewhat of an exception, and did not result in the widespread adoption of pro-casino policies as an element of local development efforts.

It was not until the 1980s that the legalization of gambling was generally regarded as a means of achieving local development and reviving a depressed local economy in the United States. In the 1980s, the legalization of gambling was employed in the United States to promote local economies through the attraction of investment, job creation, tax revenue, and tourism. The intention was to develop an economically challenged area by establishing casinos in it—much as Las Vegas, a desert city, was developed into a world-renowned resort on the basis of gambling. Under this policy of using casinos to achieve local development, casinos were introduced in Native American reservations as well as in other towns, and used as major tourist attractions.

Although casinos have often been incorporated in local development policies since the 1980s as discussed above, there are a range of differing views as to whether casinos have had a positive influence on the development of the areas in which they were built. One argument is that casinos do have a positive influence on the development of a local economy. They operate twenty-four hours a day, they create employment, and add value to an area. All of this results in a significant effect in terms of the development of the local community and its economy. Assuming an eight-hour workday for a single employee, a casino, operating around the clock, creates three times as many jobs as other businesses. The casino industry is also closely related to tourism in the local community, serving to encourage local development in socioeconomic terms. Because casinos have a positive impact on the development of a local economy, the introduction of casinos is recognized as option for local development policies.

The counter argument, however, is that casinos are not conducive to the development of a local economy. Iquest (1995) holds that Atlantic City, New Jersey had roughly 2,000 small businesses in the early days of casino development, but that number dwindled to 1,000 over a decade since the introduction of the casino industry, with consumer businesses and other smaller businesses in the local community declining. He argues that Atlantic City, in particular, came to accommodate only a casino industry and nothing else, therefore ultimately restricting the development of the city. Toalstons (1996) also estimates that the operational failure and bankruptcy of the casino industry in Louisiana left 3,500 persons unemployed and created an annual net loss of USD 20 billion for the local community, concluding that the introduction of a casino industry was a failure.

He also states that the casino industry in Illinois had a negligible impact on employment and led to a decline in retail business and overall negative results. It was also found that the tax revenue from the casino industry in South Dakota is all consumed in administrative, judicial, and legislative costs as well as social overhead capital, resulting in little substantial positive economic impact.

Carmichael (1996) and Long (1996) examined the social effect of the establishment of casinos and found that although it had a positive effect in terms of employment, it also lead to increased social costs in terms of traffic congestion and crime, and concluded that the economic development impact of casinos does not outweigh their associated social costs. Additionally, Pizam and Pokela (1985) observe that although casino development does create job opportunities, it has a negative effect in terms of crime, drug addiction, and increased living costs, thereby not ultimately enhancing the quality of life.

Put more simply, the positive impact of a casino industry on a local economy has not yet been substantiated. The limitations of casinos listed above in terms of local development, when combined with the failure of casinos built in the 1980s to have a significant impact on local development, led to a decline of casino licenses issued in the United States since the 1990s.

Recent Trends: Tendencies since the Success of the Macau Casinos

The revived global attention that casino development is receiving, and which had previously been declining as discussed above, may be ascribed to the success of the casino industry in Macau. With a dozen casinos, Macau had long been the top gambling destination in Asia. What was abnormal however was that those twelve casinos in Macau were all owned by a single person, Stanly Ho. After the city was transferred from Portugal back to China, however, the Chinese government reformed and opened up Macau's casino industry, thus ending Stanly Ho's monopoly. In January of 2002, the Macau government issued gambling licenses to the two highest bidders, with Winn Resorts of the United States and the Galaxy-Adelson consortium participating in the Macau casino industry. Consequently, in addition to the existing casinos in Macau, Sands Macau, a casino built à la Las Vegas using American capital, was opened in 2004, followed by Wynn Macau in 2006.

This new casino policy for Macau resulted in the growth of the city. Gaming revenue in Macau reached USD 5.92 billion in 2005, and exceeded USD 6.8 billion in 2006, surpassing Las Vegas to become the largest gambling center of the world. The economy of Macau suffered repeated episodes of stagnation and decline until it began posting remarkable growth: 10.1 percent in 2002, 15.6 percent in 2003, 30 percent in 2004, and 53 percent in 2005. Due to such growth, the GDP per capita of Macau exceeded USD 23,900 in 2005, surpassing that of Hong Kong.

This growth of Macau has significantly stimulated its Asian competitors. Las Vegas had long been considered the standard-bearer of casino-driven local development, but Macau was now the new model of casino-led prosperity. As a result, Singapore, where gambling had been strictly forbidden, granted licenses for casino resorts that are currently under construction, and Japan and Thailand are among other countries discreetly considering casino licensing. In those countries with existing casinos, there are new discussions to build more. In Korea, many promote building casinos wherever development is in order.

The casino-driven growth of Macau is indeed worth some attention. Is the casino, however, a surefire means of bringing about local development? The Korean government once used a casino policy to serve the purpose of local development with the Kangwon Land Casino having been built to develop an economically underdeveloped area in Gangwon. Below, we examine how great of an impact the casino actually has had on local development, by evaluating the effect of Kangwon Land Casino on the Gangwon area.

Korean Casino for Koreans: Kangwon Land Casinos

Establishment of Kangwon Land Casino

In 1967 the first group of casinos were established in Korea. These casinos were built primarily to earn foreign currency; a principle of the Korean casino policy was that all casinos are open to foreign nationals only and restricted for Korean citizens. Casinos were built at the Olympus Hotel in Incheon in 1967 and at Walker Hill Hotel in 1968, followed by the Lake Hills Hotel in 1971, KAL Hotel in Jeju in 1975, the Paradise Hotel in Busan in 1978, the Kolon Hotel in Gyeongju in 1979, and Hotel Sorak Park in 1980. In 1985, six more casinos opened in Jeju, a special tourist zone, resulting in a total of eight on the island alone. In 2006, two more in Seoul and one more in Busan were established, resulting in a total of sixteen casinos across the country. These casinos, however, were all off-limits to Korean nationals, and were intended to earn foreign currency from foreigners rather than generate local development.

In contrast to these casinos, Kangwon Land Casino in Jeongseon, Gangwondo was built to encourage the development of the local area. The region encompassing Taebaek, Samcheok, Jeongseon, and Yeongwol is the largest coalfield in Korea. Undergoing a pair of oil crises in 1973 and then in 1979, Korea switched its energy focus from oil to coal. In particular, the policy to increase coal production after the second oil crisis led to an upsurge in the number of coal mines in this region. As the oil price declined and supply stabilized on a global scale after the mid 1980s, however, the country reverted to a petro-centered energy policy, causing a rapid decline in the number of coalmines all over the country. The thirty-two mines in Gangwon Province, one after another, either shut down or reduced production levels. The precipitous decline of the coal industry, which was the sole industrial foundation of this region, led to the impoverishment of the region as a whole. The number of coalmines in Jeongseon, which was forty-four in 1988, plummeted to three by 1995, and production declined by 75 percent from 65.10 million tons to 15.76 million in that time. The number of coal industry employees dropped from 15,000 to 2,700, with these job losses leading to a population decline of over 40 percent, thus demonstrating economic devastation.

Local residents began agitating in 1994. The government finally enacted a special law to allow for the building of a casino for Koreans with the purposes of local development. This finally led to the establishment of Kangwon Land Co., Ltd. in 1998 as well as the opening of a "small" casino in October 2000, and a main casino in 2003. In an effort to build a general resort, the casino was complemented by a golf course in July of 2005 and ski slopes and a timeshare complex in December of 2006.

Financial Performance of Kangwon Land Casino

Since the opening of the "small" casino in October 2000, Kangwon Land Casino revenue reached KRW 90.9 billion in 2000, KRW 476.1 billion in 2002, and KRW 677.1 billion in 2003; surpassing KRW 847.0 billion in 2006. The small casino recorded revenues of KRW 460 billion each year, and its earnings levels were maintained at above KRW 800 billion after the opening of the main casino. This level of revenue may rank the resort well within the top 100 businesses in Korea in terms of sales, and annual net income has been recording KRW 200 billion since 2001. A debt-to-asset ratio of approximately 20 percent and a profit margin exceeding 60 percent shows that Kangwon Land Casino took a firm hold in Korea in terms of profitability and stability within the years following its foundation. Its shares, listed with the Korea Exchange and having a par value of KRW 500, are now traded somewhere around KRW 20,000, an impressive result for the investors that acquired shares in the IPO for KRW 18,500 when par value was KRW 5,000.

98 percent of these revenues are earned at the casino, with sales in the hotel accounting for a mere 2 to 3 percent of total revenue. These figures show that most visitors to Kangwon Land Casino are there to use the casino, and the success of the Kangwon Land complex is primarily due to the casino, rather than the hotel resort as a whole. That is, this Kangwon Land Casino project, designed to stimulate the economy of a former coalmine region, is exhibiting results that are more successful than expected.

Table 1. Operational Performance of Kangwon Land Casino

		2000	2001	2002	2003	2004	2005	2006
No. of visitors (persons)	Korean nationals	208,856	896,475	914,836	1,531,026	1,751,206	1,852,582	1,766,716
	Foreign nationals	493	3,115	3,862	14,314	33,524	28,977	27,030
	Total	209,349	899,590	918,698	1,545,340	1,784,730	1,881,559	1,793,746
Revenue (million Korean Won)	Casino	88,400	453,900	469,400	664,218	749,960	826,964	847,783
	Hotel	2,500	8,100	6,700	12,913	14,153	16,998	21,713
	Total	90,900	462,000	476,100	677,131	764,113	846,962	869,496
Current net income (million Korean Won)		41,200	218,300	221,000	229,690	271,233	299,089	247,936

Sources: www.kangwonland.com (2007).

The Impact of Kangwon Land Casino on the Local Economy

It is widely considered that Kangwon Land Casino has created substantially positive effects for the local economy. The effects in terms of employment and income may be deemed as the primary benefits of Kangwon Land Casino. With respect to the employment effects, in late 2000 when Kangwon Land opened its small casino, local residents and residents from abandoned coalmine areas numbered 563 and 447, respectively, out of the entire workforce of 1,134, accounting for 49.6 percent and 39.4 percent, respectively. The staff size increased to 3,101 when the main casino opened in 2003, and the numbers of local residents and residents from abandoned coalmine areas reached 1,885 and 1,553, accounting for 60.8 percent and 50.1 percent, respectively. The staff size reached 3,840 when the ski slopes opened in 2006, and the numbers of local residents and residents from abandoned coalmine areas reached 2,478 and 2,139, accounting for 65 percent and 56 percent, respectively. Thus we can conclude that the Kangwon Land complex generates an employment effect.

Kangwon Land also purchases 80 percent of its annual food materials, an amount of KRW 21.6 billion, from local providers, creating an income effect of KRW 17.2 billion. It also awards around 30 percent of its casino-related building projects to local contractors, generating an income effect of KRW 160 billion. In addition to these direct effects, the incomes of the accommodation providers, restaurants, transportation providers, and gas stations are found to have increased by 20 percent to 50 percent, highlighting Kangwon Land's positive impact on the local economy.

As for the amounts of taxes and funds paid or contributed by Kangwon Land to the central and local governments, Kangwon Land pays income tax and also contributes 10 percent of its revenues to the tourism promotion fund under casino laws. It also pays municipal taxes and contributes 10 percent of its ordinary income to the abandoned coalmine area development fund. On the whole, the amount of taxes and contributions paid by Kangwon Land reached KRW 3.80 billion in 2000, KRW 204.6 billion in 2001, KRW 187.5 billion in 2002, KRW 235.7 billion in 2003, and 285.7 billion in 2006. Kangwon Land has played a substantial role in the fundraising efforts of the central and local governments.

Discussion

Problem of Defining the Success of Casinos

As seen above, Kangwon Land Casino has successfully posted solid revenues and profits, and has also played a positive role in terms of local employment and income and tax revenue. A majority of those highlighting the success of Kangwon Land Casino, therefore, tend to promote these aspects. The fundamental purpose of establishing Kangwon Land Casino, however, was not for its own business success, but to generate local development. The whole purpose centers not around how much profit Kangwon Land makes or how much tax it pays, but around how much it encourages the growth of the local economy and to what extent it contributes to local development. Any discussion of the success or failure of Kangwon Land Casino, accordingly, requires an investigation into whether the casino has brought about a development of the area, yet most discussions seem to focus on the success of the casino business itself, its profitability, and the increase in the tax base.

Attention to a casino's profitability and revenues in determining its success is not unusual. Although the success of the Macau casinos has been discussed extensively in recent years, the discussions are focused on how much money the casino businesses make, rather than on whether Macau is undergoing genuine development and growth as a result.

The increase in the revenue and income of the casino business, however, is bound to have a particular relationship with the advancement of the local area. At the very least, any discussion of the success or failure of a casino built for the purposes of local development necessitates an observation of the impact made by the casino on the development of the area, rather than merely of the success or failure of the casino business itself.

Did Kangwon Land Casino have a Positive Impact on Local Development?

The usual focus on the revenue and profit in the discussion of the success of a casino stems from the fact that these figures are the clearest and most general indicators used for determining the success of a business. There also seems to be a lack of an undisputed definition of exactly what local development is. To make an objective assessment of local development, the criteria for evaluating local development as used by the Korean government will be used in this study. These are: 1) a population increase, 2) financial independence, 3) road infrastructure, 4) industrial population, and 5) the average land price; based on which the entire country is categorized into underdeveloped areas, urban-rural areas, and balanced development areas.

It was by these criteria that Jeongseon, Gangwondo was recognized as an underdeveloped area, prompting the development of a casino for local development purposes. Therefore, the reliance on these criteria in assessing local development may indicate whether the purpose of establishing Kangwon Land Casino has actually been achieved. These 5 criteria are neither the most important elements nor the sole requirements for local development. There could be other criteria which can be used to measure the local economic development as well. However, the Korean government used these 5 criteria to select the location of casinos and build them there. Therefore, looking into the changes of these 5 criteria in Jeongseon can serve as a basis in determining if the building of casinos was an effective tool for Korean government's local development plan.

Table 2. Population Changes in the Abandoned Coalmine Areas (in persons)

Year	Taebaek	Samcheok	Yeongwol	Jeongseon	Abandoned Coalmine Areas	Gangwon	Entire Country
1995	64,877	90,043	53,405	61,121	269,446	1,530,000	45,092,991
1996	62,489	87,370	51,809	57,362	259,030	1,531,337	45,524,681
1997	60,483	86,103	50,529	54,714	251,829	1,540,307	45,953,580
1998	59,930	85,918	50,325	53,899	250,072	1,555,483	46,286,503
1999	58,624	84,606	49,787	51,768	244,785	1,560,043	46,616,677
2000	57,067	82,255	48,437	50,631	238,390	1,559,042	47,008,111
2001	56,254	79,862	52,151	49,111	237,378	1,556,904	47,353,519
2002	55,233	77,555	45,339	51,299	229,426	1,543,665	47,615,132
2003	54,043	75,940	44,143	46,362	220,488	1,533,331	47,849,227
2004	53,384	74,577	42,618	45,633	216,212	1,528,640	48,082,163

Sources: KOSIS Statistical Information System.

_Population Growth

First of all, the population changes in Taebaek, Samcheok, Yeongwol, and Jeongseon, as well as across the entire country, are shown in Table 2.

Since 1995, each city and county area has shown a decrease in population, as have the abandoned coalmine areas as a whole. The opening of Kangwon Land in 2000 is determined to have had little effect on the decreasing tendency of the population in this region. During the same period, the population of the entire country rose from 45.09 million to 48.08 million, or by 6.6 percent, and the entire Gangwon Province region, including the abandoned coalmine areas, maintained roughly the same population at 1.53 million. As the population of the abandoned coalmine areas is steadily decreasing in contrast to that of the entire country and Gangwon Province, the tendency toward a population decrease may be recognized as limited to the abandoned coalmine areas rather than as an overall tendency. In particular, the population change in Jeongseon County, in which Kangwon Land is located, has been consistently negative since the late 1980s, with the sole exception of a brief increase in 2002, (which then reverted to a decrease in 2003). In other words, the establishment of the casino in Jeongseon County has had little impact on the tendency toward a population decrease within the Jeongseon area. The constant decrease in population despite the sizable number of jobs created by Kangwon Land suggests that the casino has had little effect on local development in terms of population.

_Local Businesses and Employees

The changes in the number of businesses in the abandoned coalmine areas are shown in Table 3.

Table 3. Changes in the Number of Businesses in the Abandoned Coalmine Areas (in businesses)

Year	Taebaek	Samcheok	Yeongwol	Jeongseon	Abandoned Coalmine Areas	Gangwon	Entire Country
1998	3,957	5,284	3,251	3,410	15,901	104,241	2,785,659
1999	4,158	5,457	3,321	3,533	16,469	109,423	2,927,330
2000	4,239	5,552	3,350	3,596	16,737	110,065	3,013,417
2001	4,286	5,470	3,342	3,595	16,693	111,610	3,046,554
2002	4,301	5,523	3,238	3,501	16,563	113,276	3,131,963
2003	4,234	5,464	3,212	3,443	16,353	115,302	3,187,916

Sources: Gangwon Statistical Bulletin, each year / KOSIS Statistical Information System.

No particular tendencies in the number of businesses were detected in each area. The number across the abandoned coalmine areas also maintained a certain level of around 16,000. On the other hand, the number across the entire Gangwon Province area climbed by 10 percent from 100,000 to 115,000 during the same period, while the figures across the entire country rose by 14 percent from 2.78 million to 3.18 million. In terms of the number of businesses, the abandoned coalmine areas stagnated, in contrast with a tendency toward an increase as seen across the country, suggesting Kangwon Land has had no particular impact on the number of businesses in the region.

The changes in the number of employees in the abandoned coalmine areas are shown in Table 7. The numbers of employees in Taebaek, Samcheok, and Yeongwol are roughly the same before and after the establishment of Kangwon Land, while the figure for Jeongseon rose by 2,000, representing a 25 percent increase. The abandoned coalmine areas as a whole showed an increase of around 2,000 persons, which may be attributed to the increase in Jeongseon County. During the same period, Gangwon Province saw a 12 percent increase in the total number of employees, whereas for the entire country this figure was 18 percent. The abandoned coalmine areas cannot seem to keep pace with Gangwon Province or the country as a whole, whereas Jeongseon County experienced a steeper increase than did either the province or the country as a whole.

In the case of the Jeongseon area, in particular, the number of businesses has remained constant at around 3,500 since the mid 1990s. The number of employees has also remained relatively constant at 13,000, until it began to increase in 2002. The number of businesses in the area, however, has been dropping since 2000, which supports the assumption that the incremental increase of

Table 4. Changes in the Numbers of Employees in the Abandoned Coalmine Areas (in persons)

Year	Taebaek	Samcheok	Yeongwol	Jeongseon	Abandoned Coalmine Areas	Gangwon	Entire Country
1998	15,921	21,748	11,508	12,270	61,444	385,097	12,416,558
1999	14,876	21,094	11,787	12,524	60,281	395,907	12,920,289
2000	15,060	21,399	12,156	13,387	62,002	405,532	13,604,274
2001	17,252	20,605	11,949	13,880	63,686	415,357	14,109,641
2002	17,478	22,117	12,232	14,035	65,862	431,064	14,608,322
2003	15,457	21,124	11,824	15,301	63,706	433,109	14,729,166

Sources: Gangwon Statistical Bulletin, each year / KOSIS Statistical Information System.

the number of employees is mostly related to Kangwon Land. Although the number of employees did rise by 20 percent or so after the opening of the casino, given the drop in the number of businesses, the numbers of businesses and employees alone are not sufficient to determine the casino's impact on local development.

_Road Infrastructure

The changes in the length of roads in Jeongseon and other abandoned coalmine areas are shown in Table 5.

The road infrastructure increased in Taebaek, Samcheok, Yeongwol, and Jeongseon. The increase in the quantity of roads, however, is an almost nationwide phenomenon, exhibited not only in the abandoned coalmine areas but also in Gangwondo and other parts of the country. As the abandoned coalmine areas, Gangwon Province, and the whole country all exhibited more than a 20 percent increase in the lengths of roads, road infrastructure cannot be considered as a direct result of the establishment of the casino.

Table 5. Changes in the Length of Roads in the Abandoned Coalmine Areas (in meters)

Year	Taebaek	Samcheok	Yeongwol	Jeongseon	Abandoned Coalmine Areas	Gangwon	Entire Country
1995	215,742	538,639	311,000	391,828	1,457,209	7,329,441	-
1996	243,915	568,554	423,900	459,428	1,695,797	7,646,208	-
1997	247,718	570,363	423,900	459,428	1,701,419	7,803,647	-
1998	251,708	578,023	418,500	446,828	1,695,059	7,831,001	-
1999	251,708	578,023	418,500	448,178	1,696,409	7,842,300	87,534,269
2000	251,708	569,883	418,500	448,178	1,688,269	7,851,912	88,775,021
2001	307,070	611,412	415,220	449,620	1,785,182	8,166,717	91,396,411
2002	299,980	611,412	417,430	499,437	1,828,259	8,162,441	96,037,098
2003	299,980	619,212	431,530	500,387	1,851,109	8,880,974	97,252,784

Sources: Gangwon Statistical Bulletin, each year / KOSIS Statistical Information System.

_Financial Autonomy

The changes in financial independence in the abandoned coalmine areas are shown in Table 6.

Table 6. Changes in Financial Independence in the Abandoned Coalmine Areas (in percentage)

Year	Taebaek	Samcheok	Yeongwol	Jeongseon	Gangwon	Entire country
1995	37.1	39.3	34.1	32.6	34	-
2000	27.2	23.9	15.9	14.7	32.4	46
2001	23.2	17.5	15.2	13.9	29.8	49.8
2002	18.6	18.7	14.1	20.8	28	55
2003	21.4	14.6	14.6	18.3	26.7	56
2004	19.5	16.7	13.8	33.19	28.9	57.2

Sources: The statistics for Taebaek, Samcheok, Yeongwol, and Jeongseon / KOSIS Statistical Information System.

The levels of financial independence of Taebaek, Samcheok, and Yeongwol have been constantly decreasing since 2000. In Jeongseon County, it had been declining until it began to increase in 2002. Despite the recent increase, however, the overall decrease exhibited up until 2002 has served to achieve levels of financial independence in 2003 comparable to those of 1995, when the region was first designated as an underdeveloped area. In Taebaek, Samcheok, and Yeongwol, the establishment of Kangwon Land may be deemed to have had little to no effect on the decrease in the level of financial independence, whereas it has had a positive effect in Jeongseon. The magnitude of the effect, however, is probably unsatisfactory. As the level of financial independence in Jeongseon however, is improving substantially, despite the regional decrease in the abandoned coalmine areas and in Gangwon Province as a whole, Kangwon Land may be regarded as having a significant impact upon the levels of financial independence in Jeongseon.

_Land Prices

Lastly, in observing land prices, average land prices are usually referred to, in general. These may then be further broken down into residential land prices and commercial land prices. It is these prices that were investigated in this study. The changes in the residential land prices in the abandoned coalmine areas, Gangwon Province, and the whole country are shown in Table 7.

From the 1995 figures, when the region was designated as an underdeveloped area, residential prices showed a 15 percent increase in Taebaek and 5 percent decreases in Samcheok and Yeongwol as of late 2004. Jeongseon County posted a 38 percent increase during the same period. Although the residential land price did rise by approximately 15 percent within a decade in Taebaek, no sub-

Table 7. Changes in Residential Land Prices in the Abandoned Coalmine Areas
(Price level at 1995 = 100)

Year	Taebaek	Samcheok	Yeongwol	Jeongseon	Gangwon	Entire country
1996	103.84	100.95	100.37	106.29	101.28	100.71
1997	104.75	101.54	101.11	107.36	102.05	100.86
1998	98.64	90.85	93.27	103.74	93.67	86.08
1999	101.02	92.08	94.57	108.33	94.93	87.85
2000	103.43	92.61	95.61	118.61	95.47	87.88
2001	108.54	92.87	95.99	127.40	95.52	88.99
2002	113.24	94.21	96.96	138.47	96.40	98.01
2003	113.80	95.93	97.29	141.78	98.35	101.35
2004	114.88	97.19	97.87	142.92	99.86	104.43

Sources: Korea Land Corporation (www.iklc.co.kr).

stantial rise in land prices was deemed to have occurred when inflation is considered. As the residential land price in Jeongseon alone is rising despite the stagnant land prices in Gangwon Province and the whole country, Kangwon Land may be considered to have had affected the average residential land price in Jeongseon County.

Changes in the commercial land prices in the abandoned coalmine areas, Gangwon Province, and the whole country are shown in Table 8. Although the average commercial land price also rose by around 8 percent in Taebaek, the effective increase is deemed to have been minimal, when considered against inflation. The commercial land prices in Samcheok, Yeongwol, and Gangwon Province showed great drops, while they rose by around 40 percent from 1995 in Jeongseon. The price is shown to have risen by 23 percent from 2000. Kangwon Land may be deemed to have affected the average commercial land price in Jeongseon.

Table 8. Changes in Commercial Land Prices in the Abandoned Coalmine Areas (Price level at 1995 = 100)

Year	Taebaek	Samcheok	Yeongwol	Jeongseon	Gangwon	Entire country
1996	104.98	100.75	100.25	107.17	100.72	100.80
1997	105.60	101.07	100.71	108.22	101.19	100.73
1998	96.86	88.41	90.77	103.01	90.97	83.52
1999	98.68	89.39	91.75	106.56	91.49	84.83
2000	100.44	89.48	92.40	116.30	91.36	84.61
2001	104.90	89.41	91.20	123.90	90.80	85.11
2002	107.94	89.68	91.63	134.60	91.54	92.50
2003	108.10	90.31	91.63	139.21	92.26	95.63
2004	108.65	90.64	91.67	142.76	92.90	98.15

Sources: Korea Land Corporation (www.iklc.co.kr).

Conclusion

This chapter investigated whether the opening of Kangwon Land Casino has, thus far, had a positive impact on the local development within the abandoned coalmine areas of Taebaek, Samcheok, Yeongwol, and Jeongseon in terms of: the population, the number of businesses and employees, road density, financial independence, and land prices. The assessment may be summarized as shown Table 9 below.

Even after the opening of Kangwon Land Casino, the size of the population has been shrinking, and the number of businesses has also been stagnating in all abandoned coalmine areas. The number of employees is increasing in Jeongseon County only, while showing no significant change in all other areas. Likewise, the level of financial independence and land prices are rising in

Table 9. Changes in Evaluation Indicators

Desc.	Population	No. of Businesses and Employees		Road Density	Financial Independence	Land Price
		No. of Businesses	No. of Employees			
Jeongseon	Decreasing	Stagnant	Increasing	Increasing	Increasing	Increasing
Abandoned coalmine areas	Decreasing	Stagnant	Stagnant	Increasing	Decreasing	Decreasing
Gangwon	Stagnant	Increasing	Increasing	Increasing	Decreasing	Stagnant
Entire country	Increasing	Increasing	Increasing	Increasing	Increasing	Stagnant

Jeongseon only, while stagnating or dropping in all other areas. The road density is rising in all areas and as road density is rising across the whole country, the development of the casino may not be seen as having caused increases in road infrastructure in the local area.

In conclusion, the development of Kangwon Land Casino, intended to encourage the local development of the surrounding abandoned coalmine areas, may be seen as having a certain level of positive influence on the local development of Jeongseon County only, which is where the casino is entirely located. During the same period in Jeongseon, no other corporate investments were made and not a single factory was built. These factors were also accompanied by a complete lack of trunk road construction or social overhead capital projects. In other words, as no other inputs aside from the building of the casino are likely to have impacted the local economy in Jeongseon, the positive effect shown above may be assumed to have been as a result of the opening of the casino.

Although the casino may be deemed to have had a positive effect on the local development of Jeongson however, there has been little to no effect in terms of local development in any other abandoned coalmine areas. A comparison between the Gangwon Province and the entire country, on the contrary, reveals a steady decline of the local economy as a whole.

The development of Kangwon Land Casino was utilized as a policy tool to drive the local development of the entire abandoned coalmine areas of Taebaek, Samcheok, Yeongwol, and Jeongseon. The current location of Kangwon Land was selected from among these four municipality candidates. In summary, it appears that although the development of Kangwon Land Casino was intended to encourage the local development of the entire underdeveloped region, the local development effect of the casino has only been felt in the area which the business is actually located, and even then to a limited degree. Furthermore, the effect is not very noticeable, and has manifested itself as marginal increases in a limited number of indicators. Although Kangwon Land Casino itself has enjoyed significant growth both in revenue and profit, the growth of the casino business appears to have had a minimal impact on local development.

The question remains as to whether the development of casinos leads to the development of the region in which they are located. Casino development may indeed bring about significant profits to a casino operation itself. It may also benefit the government in terms of increasing tax revenues. Since government in particular, has a strong tendency to regard any increase in the size of the budget as growth, an increase in the budget resulting from casinos may be recognized by the government as advancement. As discussed above, although casinos may bring substantial profits to the casino business and to the government, they do not ensure the growth of the locality. Therefore, the objective of pursuing the growth of a business or the government may provide justification for the establishment of casinos, but the imperative of local development does not appear to warrant the development of casinos; this has been amply demonstrated by the case of Kangwon Land Casino in Korea.

References

Community and Environmental Defense Services. 1996. Social and Economic Consequences of Gambling.

Gangwon-do, each year, *Gangwon Statistical Bulletin*.

Taebaek-si, Samcheok-si, Jeongseon-gun, Yeongwol-gun, *A Statistical Yearbook*.

Burros, J. 1996. Likely Tourism Impacts of Indian Gambling, *Economics Research Associates*.

Carmichael, B., D., Peppard and F., Boudreau. 1996. Mega-Report on My Doorstep; Local Resident Attitudes toward Foxwoods Casino and Casino Gambling on nearby Indian Reservation Land, *Journal of Travel Research* 34(3).

Chae, Y. 2001. A Study on the Feature in Policy-Process of Small Casino, *Journal of Tourism Policy* 7(2).

Choi, S. and H., Hwang. 2006. An Evaluation of the Effects of Kangwon Land Establishment Policy on the Regional Development of Closed Mine Vicinities, *Journal of Public Administration* 44(2).

Chung, K. 1998. Market Analysis of the Casino Industry in Korea, *Journal of Tourism Science* 22(1).

Eadington, W.R. 1995. The Emergence of Casino Gaming as a Major Factor in Tourism Markets, In R. Butler and D. Pearce. eds. *Change in Tourism: People, Places, Processes*, New York: Routledge.

_______. 1996. The Legalixation of Casinos: Policy Objectives, Regulatory Alternatives and Cost/Benefit Considerations, *Journal of Travel Research* 34(3).

Han, K. 2001. A Study on Promotion of the Abandoned Mining Areas Resort Complex, Kangwon Land, *Journal of Tourism and Information* 8.

Iquest. 1995. The Negative Impact of Casino, Legalized Gambling as a Strategy for Economic Development, *United States Gambling Study*.

Kwon, B. and J., Lee. 2000. The Research of Resident Mind in Che-Ju Area about Casino Admission Allowance for Natives, *Journal of Tourism* 15(2).

Lee, C. and B., Lee. 2003. Characteristic Differences between Kangwon Land Casino Visitors with Respect to the Level of Involvement, *Journal of Tourism Science* 27(2).

Lee, C. and C., Park. 1996. Analysis of the Economic Impact of the Korean Casino Industry, *Journal of Tourism Science* 27(2).

Lee, C. and S., Kang. 2004. A Longitudinal Study of Resident's Perceptions towards Kangwon, *Journal of Hotel management* 13(1).

Lee, S. 1997. Analysis of the Factor of Geographical Distance Influencing Interorganizational Relations between Tourism Promotion Organizations and the Riverboat Casino Industry, *Journal of Tourism and Development* 6.

_______. 1998. A Study for Induction and Problems of Casino Industry in the Time of IMF, *Journal of Tourism and Development* 8.

Long, P.T. 1996. From the Guest Editor, *Journal of Travel Research* 34(3).

McIntosh, W. and Goeldner. 1990. Tourism Principles, Practices, Philosophies, NY: John Wiley & Sons, INC.

Perdue, L. and Kang. 1999. Boomtown Tourism and Resident Quality of Life: The Marketing of Gaming to Host Community Residents, *Journal of Business Research* 44(3).

Pizam, A. and J., Pokela. 1985. The Perceived Impacts of Casino Gambling on a Community, *Annals of Tourism Research* 12(2).

Sohn, D. 2002. The Reality and Development Plan of Korean Casino Industry, *Journal of Tourism Research* 14.

Shin, D. 2003. A Review on the Activation Plan of the Domestic Casino Industry, *Journal of Industry Economics*.

Toalston, A. 1996. Baptist Press News Archive: Louisiana Voters Weighing State's Gambling Addiction, July 11.

Wicks, B.E. and A.N., Kathryn. 1996. Urban Riverboat Casino Planning: Including the African American Perspective, *Journal of Travel Research* 34(3).

Yoon, J. 1998. Marketing Strategy for Casino Industry in Korea, *Journal of Tourism Management* 2.

Part III

Citizen Participation

Chapter 6 |

Cyber Citizen Participation and e-Government

KI-SHIK LEE

Introduction

We are currently experiencing the release of new products and services based on information technologies such as on-line games, remote medical treatment, e-Learning, e-Science and so on. Such developments result in speeding up digital convergence and include the unity between cable and wireless networks, unity in IT, BT, and NT and the living base extension of RFID sensing technology.(Mostefaoui, Maamar and Giaglis, 2008; Theng and Duh, 2008). In particular, things and space are sophisticated by web 2.0 extensions, UCC activations, and new trends which pursue participation and public ownership are being formed because real-time collection of information is possible at anytime and anywhere.

Since 1987, administrative informatization has been introduced through a national basic electronic network project, and the Kim Young-Sam Government (1993–1998) constructed an internet super-highway project and promoted the informatization of Korean society on this basis. The Kim Dae-Jung Government continued this trend and selected 11 tasks of electronic government in order to establish a foundation for electronic government. The Roh Moo-Hyun Government (2003–2008) during its administration then selected 31 tasks of the electronic government under the notion of 'transparent and well-functioning government' to promote electronic government as basis of government innovation.

Originally, the meaning of electronic government was to extend the concepts which stemmed from electronic banking services first. That is, as ATM, plastic cards and national network services made banking work processing easier, the electronic government was seen as a means of making the communication between government and citizens easier and faster (NPR, 1993; Jeong Chungsik, 2007). Accordingly, electronic government can be viewed as a government which effectively executes the administrative matters of each administrative organization and also between people and companies by using information technologies. Thus there is a realization of the so-called client-oriented democratic government which efficiently delivers citizens' standpoints and receives feedback information. Therefore, because electronic government should realize client-oriented democratic government, it is important that citizens' opinions are taken into account when executing administration.

The citizen participation dealt with in this study is based on such an idea. Thus, it attempts to take full consideration of citizens' opinions in policy making which thus makes electronic democracy which is based on direct democratic systems, possible. Additionally, the possibility of administrative innovations which are obtained through citizens' internet participation are expected by surpassing the limits of a representative democratic system which is involved in scale politics. In the future, because the internet is more economical than other media outlets when taking into account aspects such as public relations and the collection of public opinions, it is expected to be used as a place for communication between the government and citizens.

This study attempts to understand citizen participation from a perspective of electronic government. Cyber-Citizen Participation (CCP hereafter), is said to induce citizens to take part in the policy processes of the central and/or local government by using the medium of cyberspace.

Theoretical Background

Discussions related to citizen participation date all the way back to ancient politicians. In the 4th century B.C., Perikles pointed out that discussion among citizens regarding political action were inevitable. (Thucydides, 1998). The importance of Cyber-Citizen Participation (CCP) can be explained by two reasons; political and administrative significance of citizen participation, and trust between the government and citizen.

The first and most important aspect of citizen participation is that it can make strong democracy possible. In the event that a nation's problems and issues are solved via citizen participation, strong democracy can come true. Like Barber(1984)'s assertion, a strong democracy is realized not by private use, but rather by the process of men and women of all ages discussing issues together, and through this process, every citizen finding their common humanity. Thinking from a public officials' standpoint, they can seek citizen-oriented policies because they help citizens understand unfamiliar policies by explaining these policies to them, and in the process take citizens' standpoints into consideration.

CCP makes client-oriented administration possible. Citizens can help public officials persuade and recognize their own preferences via their participation. We view the client-oriented administration as 'providing administrative services appropriate to clients' perceived values and demands. Thus CCP makes citizen's input into the policy system possible, and this input is the most effective way to make the government know what its citizens want.

From the government's standpoint, CCP helps the government be trusted. The problems related to trust represent an important issue when considering how to manage a modern nation. This is because, in many cases, a lack of trust in the government causes the failure of policy. The mutual understanding between citizens and the government which results from citizens participation, thus increases the public's trust in the administration (Yun Sang-Oh, 2003: 82).

CCP also influences the accumulation of social capital. In the event that citizen participation works well, a horizontal network and better information retrieval between the government and citizens can be formed, and the distrust between both of them can be decreased (Putnam, 2000). At this point, citizen participation makes the trust between citizens, the government and the cooperative network of regulations possible.

Theoretically, there can be various degrees of cyber participation. Im Kwang-Hyeon(2002) surveyed people who visited the civil affairs office in their local city or the county hall in order to estimate the maturity of the electronic government. His analysis showed that people with public complaints value the electronic government project in general. In particular, they recognized that the search of relevant sectors and convenience of use got better. Yun Sang-Oh (2003) evaluated to what extent the level of realization of the electronic government matured by. He selected 4 models in order to measure the maturity of the electronic government from the viewpoint of citizen participation, and analyzed 40 central administrative organizations in Korea. The analysis showed that the level of citizen participation was insufficient. This result pointed out that public availability of all administrative information and a change in understanding for citizen participation were needed in order to raise the level of citizen participation. Ryu He-Yeon (2003) analyzed the factors which influenced the usage of electronic government services. The analysis showed that technical factors, marketing factors, and communication factors were important. Marketing factors are called public relationship and motivation. Jeong Cheol-Hyeon (2004) looked into the factors which influenced users when they were using the electronic government web site. The results showed that usage of the web site was influenced by site access, convenience and users' informatization level. The study particularly suggested the importance of users' informatization levels. Jo Seok-Ju and Kang In-Seong (2006) suggested that the level of citizen participation and improvement in local autonomous entities were also important. They analyzed the actual conditions of citizen participation systems which were managed in many cities and districts, and examined the level of citizen participation through a survey. Their results showed that citizen participation is conducted by various methods ranging from on-line to off-line, and that the level was 'common'. Ryu Hyeon-Suk (2008) analyzed Korean participation in the electronic government sites and recognition. The analysis showed that even if Korean people regarded it as an important mechanism to search for administrative information and to express political problems, they did not use the site actively. Accordingly, the study concluded that the on-line project of the Korean electronic government was a partial success.

Table 1 shows the contents of detailed effects on services for citizens provided by the electronic government in Korea. Most participation systems including opinion surveys and the previous notices of legislation have high democratic value. Especially, it shows the people's suggestion system and the referendum are very effective.

Table 1. Major Methods of Cyber-Citizen Participation

Methods	Pariticipants*			Effects	Democratic Implementation
Public Survey	A	B	C	Middle	Critical
Discussion Room	A	B	C	Middle	Critical
A Noticed Board	A	B	C	Low	Critical
Notice of Lawmaking	A	B	C	Low	Critical
Supply of Information	A		C	Middle	Very Critical
Public Hearing	A	B	C	Middle	Critical
Official Notice	A		C	Low	Critical
Education	A	B	C	Low	Critical
Advisory Committee			C	Middle	Critical
Panel	A		C	Middle	Critical
Workshop	A		C	High	Critical
National Suggestion	A	B	C	High	Very Critical
Vote	A	B	C	High	Very Critical

Sources: Reconstruct based upon Jo Seok-Ju and Kang In-Seong (2006).
* A: Ordinary Citizen with Interests B: Ordinary Citizen Without Interests C: Public Representatives Without interests.

Structure of Cyber Citizen Participation

The structure of cybercitizen participation (CCP) consists of the intention, method and role of participation, and the factors affecting citizen participation.

Intention of Participation

The details and structure of participation rely on the people's will for cyber participation. Some people connect with the civil affairs site in order to access services like obtaining a certificate of the resident registration, and others use the notice board to suggest their opinions regarding policies. Some people also take part in the cyber discussion site, Agora, and so on to state their own opinions, and perhaps even finally to practice them. Of course, we can also see people who connect to the site just to post, rather than to access for civil affairs services or actively participate in current problems.

The intention or purpose of citizen participation can be divided into a two by two table according to issues such as activeness or passiveness and whether to pursue public profit or private profit (Fugure 1). First of all, they show the expression of passive/negative concerns about the details issued off-line and on-line. This set belongs to type IV in the next Figure. It is a type where they express their own opinions through a notice board and ripples, but they come into line with others generally. Sometimes, they express their opinions in order to break up their stress or to increase self-efficiency.

Type II is a type that citizens use to express positive/independent concerns over the details issued off-line and on-line. It related to their own profit. For example, it includes cases where they are asked to state their opinions about dissolving a greenbelt or developing land for housing lots. Because this case is related to citizens' profit, it changes to a new problem through its cooperation with non-government organizations (NGOs)

Type III is a type that formed in order to improve public political processes or administrative transparency on the basis of others' opinions without reference to their own interest in the details issued through off-line and on-line. Citizens involved in this type take part in policies which fall into line with others related to political issues or local issues. Most on-line users belong to this type.

Type I is a type where citizens state their opinions based on their own judgment rather than others' opinions of administrative processes and political efficiency. This type is not common.

Figure 1. The Types of Citizen Participation

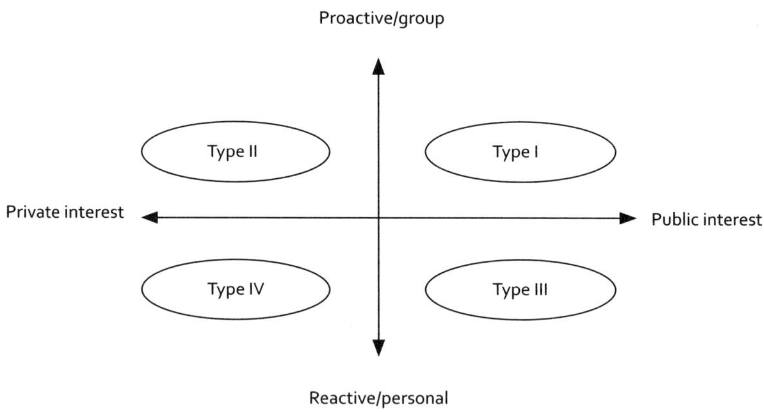

Methods of Cyber Citizen Participation

The methods of CCP are at variance. Participation by internet is a common point, and the details are as follows.

1) E-mail, Internet Homepage: When citizens put questions to the government (local autonomous entity) by E-mail or by using Q&A and the notice board of Homepage, the government (local autonomous entity) answers them. They also answer by e-mail or by using the notice board.

2) Policy forum, citizen forum: It is the case where citizens take part in policies through policy forums and citizen forums on line. In this case, there are incentive systems including rewards to activate participation. For example, Incheon-City provides merchandise bonds for citizens to participate in forums.

3) Cyber-national participation: It is a method of using e-people services (www.epeople.go.kr) in cyberspace. The Korean government provides one-stop services so that the people can handle filing petitions, proposals, reports entailing administrative agencies' unlawful acts and administrative judgment on this site. First of all, in the case of petition services, citizens can apply for petitions on line and receive the results on line. The area of petition application is varies widely and includes demands for questions and explanation about administrative affairs and unreasonable acts. The cases which have been managed number around 13,900 as of August 2008 in Korea. The Proposal service is said to be where citizens hand over creative opinions and plans to the chief of an administrative agency in order to improve policies, administrative systems, and operation. In the event that its details belong to petition, it will transfer to the petition service to be managed. The proposal service can be conducted behind closed doors as well as in public. The case of corruption reporting involves the events where public officials abused their positions and authority, and broke laws

in their own interest or in the interest of a third person. If an Anti-Corruption and Civil Rights Commission (ACCRC) takes over the statement, it will be brought to an examination group through a fact-finding process in 60 days (possible to extend by 30 days) and the result will be released in 60 days. On-line administrative judgments are managed in order to help citizens demand a judgment and check the process and result easily and conveniently in contrast to the existing administrative judgment process which is conducted via post. Citizens can receive answers to questions related to administrative judgments in real-time and also take part in policy discussion. Policy discussion consists of electronic public hearings, participation in forums, and surveys which thereby allow citizens to actively suggest their opinions when deciding policies. Every citizen can state their opinions, and discuss various views through policy forums.

4) Petition information service: Citizens can use the call center (number 110) for government petition information. This call center unifies call numbers for government petition information in order to solve the problem of citizens not understanding the complicated government structure and call number systems. If anyone dials 110, a special counselor will give them advice, and the citizen can receive the government's service without needing to know about the government's organizational systems.

5) Electronic polls and Electronic elections: Recently, voter turnout in general elections as well as local elections is around 20 percent. This level of participation is regarded as a general and universal result rather than a particular and temporary phenomenon which results from political distrust and difficult economic conditions. Accordingly, in the event that electronic elections become possible, voter turnout will likely be higher. In January 2005, 'a roadmap for promoting electronic polls' was presented, and con-

sistent concern has been given to it until now. Like this, one of core measure of CCP can be deemed electronic polls and electronic elections.

Roles of Cyber Citizen Participation

Citizen participation plays many roles in cyberspace. First of all, it plays a role of realizing e-Democracy. The fact that citizens directly take part in policies through cyberspace demonstrates the possibility of e-Democracy. E-Democracy also increases the efficiency of administration, reliability, and transparency by using cyberspace. Seoul City (Gangnam-gu) executes direct and practical citizen participation in the process of e-information, e-interaction, and e-integration through the cyber citizen participation systems. This demonstrates a grass-roots democracy movement which we can assume highly valued participation, self-government and the possibility of citizen participation and cooperation, thereby realizing true local democracy.

CCP makes the innovation of petition services possible. The so-called G4C (Government for Customer) is considered a part of it. G4C is a project to change existing systems where citizens (the people) directly visit the petition windows of public offices, to electronic petition windows (portal sites), and then finally connecting with main administrative organizations (Jeong Chung-Sik, 2007: 228). This project is expected to increase the efficiency of citizen participation.

CCP plays a role in the potential of e-Governance. Regarding citizen participation in cyberspace, it is possible to have a conversation with the government, the mayor, and citizens and also to activate e-Governance. Governance is related to issues such as 'the government's roles and operating methods', and it is a process through which the interested parties (local inhabitants) make agreements by way of self-regulating conversation, negotiation and mediation with special goals (Jessop, 2000; UNGC, 2006). Currently, it is possible to make a governance mechanism with information and communication technology in cyberspace and to form de-centralized networks through agreement and mediation. We can move beyond these limitations of a representative system by using e-governance

The reliability of administration and an increase in transparency are possible through feedback of the CCP. One of the core benefits of cyber citizen participation is that so-called feedback is accomplished due to informing the results of participation to local inhabitants by internet. It is not too much to say that this type of feedback is very important. Citizens can recognize how much their opinions are taken into account and whether they connect with practical policies (systemization), to satisfy their efficacy (Song Kyeong-Jae, 2007). The fact that residents receive certain information regarding local problems from the local government displays the reliability of the local government and contributes to the accumulation of local social capital which helps to increase mutual benefits among citizens.

Lastly, the establishment of policy network is possible. The increase of on-line citizen participation makes the establishment of policy networks between parties interested in certain issues possible. In the meantime, the problem with policy networks was that their transaction costs were high, but, through on-line participation, the transaction costs nearly comes to zero, however the efficiency of participation is doubling.

Two Cases of Cyber Citizen Participation in Korea

Because the cases of CCP in Korea are almost the same regardless of central or local organizations, this study plans to examine Gangnam-gu, which is located in the Seoul metropolitan government (Gangnam-gu office) and Incheon Metropolitan City (Incheon City), and suggest the stage of participation according to policy process.

Gangnam-District of Seoul Metropolitan City

Gangnam-gu office has collected local inhabitants' opinions through internet since September 2001. Gangnam-gu office understands the cyber citizen participation system (http://esurvey.gangnam.go.kr reference date August 16, 2008) from the viewpoint of e-democracy and points out that inhabitants directly take part in administration to decide issues. Gangnam-gu office executes policies many inhabitants want by collecting inhabitants' opinions by internet. For example, the result of surveying inhabitants is reflected by the decision of a subway station name, of installing CCTV in back streets as well as making a budget, and the cases extend to 500 cases.

Figure 2 Collecting Process of Inhabitants' Opinions

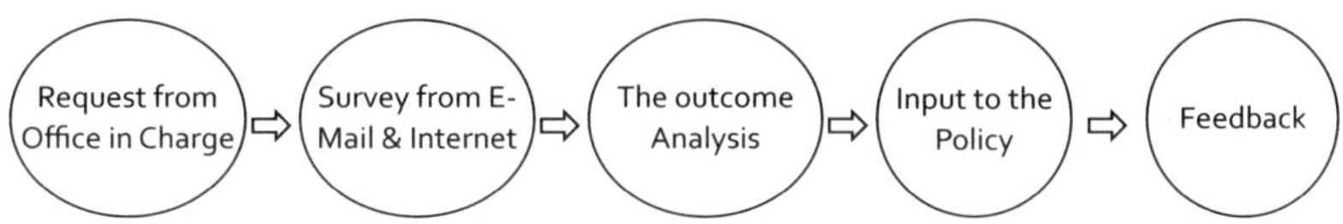

In the process of collecting inhabitants' opinions, the questions are set up through the citizen participation system which begins when a responsible sector requests an examination as you see in Figure 2. After analyzing answers for a specific period, the results are reflected in policies. The policies reflected reflow to inhabitants through public notice. The CCP system of Gangnam-gu office collects opinions through the policy discussion room as well as through e-mail or surveys. It is possible to state opinions freely and to appoint the discussion subject. Gangnam-gu Office's cyber-citizen participation structure is composed of administrative participation, the room for policy discussion and the room of suggestion as seen Figure 3.

The specialties of CCP in Gangnam-gu office are as follows (Song Kyeing-Jae, 2007). First of all, direct and practical citizen participation is possible. And not only feedback in the process of policy execution exists but also participants are given incentives to participate. Especially, important items are feedback and incentives. Feedback related to inhabitants' behavior provides efficiency and satisfaction, and offers the possibility to reproduce participation positively. Incentives are intended to give material benefits to cyber participants. Incentives have a large effect on inhabitants' recognition and behaviors, and can cause positive behavior.

Figure 3. Gangnam-gu Office' Cyber-Citizen Participation Structure

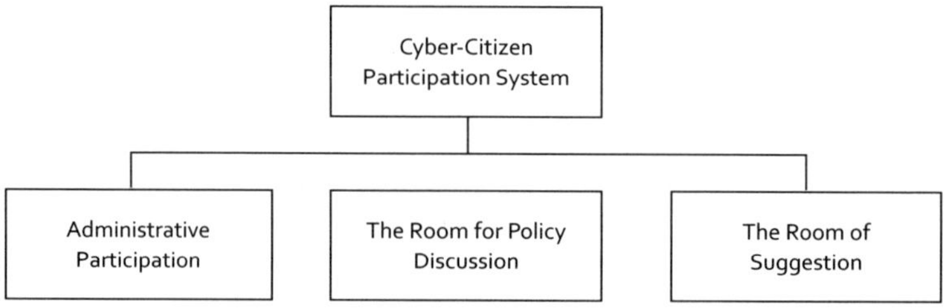

Incheon Metropolitan City

Incheon Metropolitan City (Incheon City) opens administrative information to citizens online, and induces citizen participation.

1) *Public access to various government information*: Incheon-City opens information through various on-line channels to guarantee citizens right to know and to secure the transparency of operating policies. At first, Incheon City executed the information open system which was a measure taken to ensure that every self-governing organization operates according to the act of information open (statute number of 8871) in Korea. Incheon City provides citizens with new information related to policies through 'Incheon News'. It provides public procurement information and employment information as well as information about buses, food, development and events. Namely, it also offers information regarding the opening of bid information to the results in detail. In case of employment information, it provides national examination information, employment information as well as information about Incheon. The announcement and public notice related to Incheon's policies work well. Incheon City provides Incheon's policies and news about citizens through Internet broaD.C.asting. Especially, Internet broaD.C.asting shares UCC that inhabitants made through UCC square, funny pictures and so on. And, Incheon's culture, theme and cultural lectures are conducted. An internet newspaper introduces Incheon to citizens. It contains policies, field pictures and cartoons. Finally, Incheon City helps citizens to contact the existing publications through eBook. Citizens can read periodicals published at Incheon Development Institute as well as white papers, and policy reports on line.

2) *Various opportunities of CCP*: Incheon City provides various online methods to participate in civic policies. Major online methods are citizens' voice, citizens' suggestions, the citizen discomfort report center, debating place, survey, events, blog forum, cafes and so on. First of all, the section of 'citizens' voice' is a notice board which aims to collect citizens' opinions (question/proposal/suggestion) related to Incheon's policy, and finally to reflect them to civic policies. Incheon City also listens to various citizens' voices in the sections of 'Let's praise' and the free board. In the case of citizens' suggestions, it collects citizens' suggestions for Incheon's improvement. But, the petitions, private opinions and so on are deleted from the site; the only thing that remains are suggestions. Incheon City operates the citizen discomfort reports center. It collects information related to sources of discomfort for citizens' which include traffic, regulations, official corruption, contamination, industrial difficulties and excessive budgets. Incheon City receives 8,100 cases of traffic problems a day as of August, 2008. And in case of a debating place, citizens can freely debate mutual opinions about the specific subject there. The result of debating is the basis of political action for citizens. In any event, it provides good debaters with incentives which allow them to buy products with mileage. Moreover, it uses surveys as data for the open policy. Many opinions are collected through Blogs and cafes. If one becomes a member in Incheon City Homepage, a blog is given automatically.

How to Realize Effective Cyber Citizen Participation

CCP in the Policy Process

CCP can be helpful in various ways at different steps along the policy process. In terms of decentralization which here means narrowing the gap between policy makers and citizens, CCP is one of the most effective methods of enhancing citizen participation. Local governments in Korea have experimented with CCP practices alongside of the typical policy process as follows.

1) *Phase of agenda setting*: In the phase of setting up an agenda, information is given, or it provides information to citizens, and related opinions are collected. As the cyber opinion collection window, Seoul metropolitan government, Incheon Metropolitan City, Ulsan Metropolitan City, Gangwon-do and Gyeongsangbuk-do operate the section of 'we expect a self-governing entity'. The patterns of consultation that each self-governing entity uses consist of 'meeting with a local government head', 'the political survey through internet and questions' and 'the cyber policy debating place'. For example, through 'Saturday's conversation with the mayor (Seoul government), 'cyber mayor room (Incheon City), Internet surveys (Gwangju City), and the citizen participation budget system (Chungcheongnam-do), opinions are collected or suggested. In this phase, the active windows that citizens can participate through, positively consist of 'imaginary suggestion', 'debating place (Seoul government)', 'citizen suggestion (Incheon City)', 'citizen inspection application system' (Gwangju City, Daejeon City) and Internet inhabitant participation (Gyeongsanbuk-do).

2) *Phase of forming policies*: The phase of forming policies is a step that issues selected build up of policies. In this phase, through

'civic political news' (Seoul government), approval of documents opening room (Ulsan City), uploading the budget to the internet (Gangwon-do), civic political news (Incheon City), internet petition monitor (Gyeongsandnam-do), the policy details are open. Also, through various commission systems, cyber policy debating (Chungcheongbuk-do) and political agreement is made up. The active systems to form policies consist of internet opinion surveys (Seoul government), questionnaires (Incheon City), district's present opinion survey and public budget hearings (Jeonju City). Internet channels as a means of forming policy are gradually advancing. Seoul metropolitan government executes Panel Surveys, Brainstorming, Mystery Shoppers, Monitoring Surveys, Customer Analysis, Customer Satisfaction, Home use Tests, Focus Group Interviews and Mail Surveys for opinion surveys.

3) *Phase of executing policies*: In this phase, every self-governing entity provides relevant information through the public administrative information systems. Besides the public information system, civic political news (Seoul government), petition corruption report center (Daegu City), mailing letters service (Incheon City), Friday's petition with citizens (Daejeon City), excess budget report center (Ulsan City), honorary environmental inspector (Gyeongsangbuk-do) and environmental Sinmoongo (Gyeongsangnam-do) are involved. The active pattern of citizen participation is made up by unforced participation of volunteers and honorary inspectors. It consists of citizen discomfort report center (Incheon City) and citizen inspector system in large government supply construction.

4) *Phase of evaluating policies*: In case of this phase, relevant information involves white papers, annual bulletins, and public information. The policy monitoring system makes many agreements possible. For example, through various 'cyber monitoring systems' which include citizen monitors (Seoul government), self-

governing monitors (Incheon City), cyber route monitors, female monitors (Gangwon-do) and policy monitors (Chungcheongbuk-do), citizen participation is made up in the evaluating stage. The more active participation patterns involve internet opinion surveys, the more the people's satisfaction survey and ombudsman.

Advancing e-Government

Effective CCP for the development of e-government are as follows. First of all, public information should increase in order to activate participation in cyberspace. Korea established the law regarding the opening of public information in public organizations on 13th December 1996, but it lacks in many ways related to the viewpoints of inquirers of public information. And, it is necessary for public officials in charge to maintain a positive attitude toward public information. Second, proper incentives for people who participate in political measures online must be provided. The government should provide material benefits including 'merchandise bonds' and symbolic benefits including 'citizen prizes' for people who have offered innovative ideas. Several self-governing entities execute the incentive system, but, the extension of it is needed. Third, it is necessary to make the citizen participation site easy to use. To the latter, it is needed to establish a user-friendly system and to prepare for systematic equipment to update the relevant site consistently. Finally, we should stop abusing others; curses to obstruct public moral, criticisms without truth or suggesting contents limited to one's own benefit would be examples of such behavior. In Korea, in case of presenting same contents over three times without proper conditions, the organization can neglect or end it. But, we should restrain the activities pertaining to the purpose of cyber citizen participation before such forced regulations.

In addition to these, there are five factors largely influencing CCP. The first factor is information infrastructure. As information infrastructure is being established, cyber citizen participation will increase. Considering that subscribers of the super-highway internet number around 147,000,000, the 7th highest among OECD member states (KADO, 2008), we can assume that most homes are equipped with Internet. The second factor is the on-line attachment. Participants in cyberspace can have more of an online attachment than non-participants. Online attachment is considered as an inclination and will that an internet user does not separate virtual space from one's self. The third factor is the concrete conditions and contexts in cyberspace. Context can cause a range and intensity of participation. The complexity and uncertainty of the issues in cyberspace can create other problems as well. The fourth factor is the purpose of participation. The purpose of participation in cyberspace can influence its contents and roles. In addition, the range and intensity of participation can be diversified according to citizens' interest in cyberspace. The last variables which influence CCP are related to participants' individual characteristics. They seem to be related to social and economic resources like education, income level, vocational position as well as innate traits such as gender, age, and health.

Limitation of CCP

Like other policy tools, CCP is of course not without its own limitations. The policy implications which can be deduced from this study are as follows.

First, we should pay attention to the fact that CCP may obstruct the efficiency of political measures. Policy postponement can occur on purpose or accidently via citizen participation. In the process of collecting citizens' opinions, there are many cases in which opinions are divided into many directions. Thus policies are postponed or efficiency is obstructed.

Second, CCP also offers a potential for biased results in that only some internet users' opinions are reflected in policies. This is due to the fact that participants in cyberspace are able to use the internet and have the necessary skills to operate information infrastructure. But, because most users involved are relatively young, or possibly biased, they cannot represent entire population. We should also pay attention to the fact that the opinions of people who are not concerned can be reflected in policies. It is important to collect serious opinions of people who sense problems through cyber participation. In this respect CCP can also serve as a method of simply decreasing participants stress. Additionally we should also consider the possibility of limited cyber participants because the elderly population only has limited capability when it comes to expressing their opinions online when compared to the younger generations.

Third, it is important to enforce the connection between online and offline. Actually, offline participation cannot help but to be restricted. As a result of the restrictions of time and space, many people's participation can be restricted with the exception of experts, relevant persons, and NGO groups (Jo Seokju and Kang Inseong, 2006). In this respect, online citizen participation is very beneficial in helping to overcome the restrictions of time and space. In this sense, logically there should not be any differences between opinions and directions of citizen participation online and offline. The interest and the directions experts and relevant persons have should be somewhat aligned with online participants. But, actually, because the young lead online participation, a stronger connection between them is needed, so the basis of CCP can be damaged.

Fourth, basically, because CCP offers anonymity, we should be careful because anonymity decreases participant's sense of responsibility. Cyber participants are increasing, but the power of participants can be weaken due to their anonymity, and in the case of the self-governing entities, responsibility can decrease when collecting opinions in cyberspace, mostly because we don't know the exact response of the self-governing entities. Most inhabitants also use anonymous online identifications, so they lack responsibility for their opinion.

In spite of such these restrictions, CCP offers the possibility of serving as a new self-governing and an administrative paradigm. Internet makes connections between various people possible by allowing participants to overcome the existing social limits and barriers on the basis of anonymity. Through this connection, they suggest their own meaningful opinions and suggestions and interact with each other, sometimes, to make a decision. Because each inhabitant has a different relationship, if they state their own opinions regarding a specific subject online, these opinions are proliferated. As such, in case not to extend to the social problem, it is impossible for inhabitants to deny the vertical order and the typical role distribution and to connect with other groups in the horizontal relation. We can better recognize such relationships through the practice of internet debates. Internet debates have been advancing to the extent that they now satisfy users' needs and increase citizen participation. Consequently the platform through which participation occurs results in an increase of debates and the patterns of comments become more varied, with many people increasingly participating in the online debates.

Lastly, cyber-security and individual privacy should be protected in order to secure CCP. Cyberspace should be protected from danger, threats, and crimes, and inhabitants' privacy should not be damaged by the various data and information which comes out during the process of cyber participation. Thus each individual's privacy should not be disturbed during the processes of opening and participating in the various channels of information.

References

KADO, 2008. 2008 White Papers, Korea Agency Digital Opportunity and Promotion.

UNGC. 2006. Developmnet Plan for United Nation Goverance Center, Reserarch Report. United Nations Governace Center.

Barber, B. 1984. *Strong Democracy: Participatory Politics for a New Age,* Barkeley: University of California Press.

Brants, K, M., Huizenga and van M.R. 1996. The Canals of Amsterdam: And Exercise in Local Electronic Democracy, *Media, Culture and Society* 18(2): 233–47.

Im, K. 2002. The Evaluation of eGovernment's Mature Level through Service Quality, *Korean Journal of Public Analysis and Evaluation* 12(2).

Jeong, C. 2004. The Influencing Factors on the Use of eGovernment Web Site, *The Korean Public Administration Journals* 13(4): 122–47.

_______. 2007. *e-Government,* Seoul Economy Management Press.

Jessop. 2000. Governance Failure, In G., Stoker ed. *The New Politics of British Local Governance,* St. Martin Press.

Jo, S. and I., Kang. 2006. Diagnosis of Local Resident's Public Participation and Directives, *The Research Report, 2006–09*. Korea Research Institute for Local Administration.

Lee, K. 1998. Institutional Aspects for Opening Government Information in the Electronic Environment, *Korean Public Administration Review* 32(4): 119–38.

Mostefaoui, S.K., Z., Maamar and G.M., Giaglis. 2008. *Advances in Ubiquitous Computing: Future Paradigms and Directions,* IGI Publishing.

NPR (National Performance Review). 1993. *Reengineering through Information Technology,* Availale at Website.

Putnam, R. 2000. *Bowling Alone: the Collapse and Revival of American Commuity,* New York: Simon & Schuster.

Ryu, H. 2003. The Mode of Interest Intermediation in Policy Process: For the Comparison and Integration of Three Perspectives, *The Korean Public Administration Journals* 12(3).

_______. 2008. Online Participation and Perception Based on D.C.LEAR Model, *The Korean Public Administration Journals* 17(1).

Seo, J. 2000. The Measure of Informatization Level of Local Residents Based on Information Literacy, *Korean Public Administration Review* 34(1): 309–26.

Song, K. 2007. Building Local E-Governance and Possibility of Civil Participation e-Democracy, *Discouse 201* 9(4): 105–39.

Theng, Y.L. and H., Duh. 2008. *Ubiquitous Computing: Design, Implementation and Usability,* (Premier Reference Source) IGI Publishing.

Thucydides. 1998. *The Peloponnesian War,* Lattimore S. Trans., Hackett Publishing Company.

Westby, J.R. 2000. *International Guide to Cyber Security,* American Bar Association.

Yun, S. 2003. A Study on eGoverment and Civil Participation, *Korean Policy Science Review* 7(1): 79–104.

Chapter 7 |

Science or Citizen Participation?: A Case Study of Water Fluoridation Program in South Korea

MINAH KANG AND DOOL-SUN KIM

Introduction

Health and environment are sectors where local residents have strong desires to participate due to the fact that everyone is generally very concerned with their health (Lee, 2002; Kang et al., 2005). Compared to national policy issues that typically relate to philosophical or ethical points of dispute, local policy decision-making related to issues such as city planning, landfill site selections, or regional health planning, can serve as a window of opportunity for citizen participation. These are opportunities where individual interests can be reflected in policy decisions with respect to real-life matters that are closely related to the daily life of residents (Herson and Bolland, 1990). However, policies related to health and environmental problems are often considered fields that are difficult for residents to take a meaningful part in. This is due to the complexity of the problems, as well as the general population's lack of expertise and/or ignorance regarding such issues. In this study, we examined the role of citizen participation with respect to regional public health policies through a case study of the water fluoridation program in Korea.

City water fluoridation programs came into operation during the 1950s for the first time in the United States. This program consists of adding fluorine to tap water in an effort to prevent dental caries. The program has now been implemented in 61 countries all over the world, including countries in Europe, North America and South-east Asia (Kim et al., 2007). A number of western countries, and the World Health Organization, encouraged implementation of the program as a major public oral health program after the preventive effects of fluorine against dental caries were identified through repeated studies. In Korea, the program was implemented in the early 1980s.

Recently however, environmental groups and ecologists have raised questions related to the safety of fluorine with respect to the environment and the human body. Some doubters claim that the fluorine may be harmful, or more specifically can lead to cancer. For this reason, some operational decisions of the program have been reversed or delayed due to the intense resistance of civic groups and local residents. While its scientific effects are not certain, citizen participation has tremendously affected the implementation of the program.

Using the case of the fluorine program, this study explores the development of citizen participation models as decentralization reforms were introduced in the early 1990s. Specifically, this study focuses on the dynamics between the local government and local residents throughout the process of decision-making. To elucidate the aforementioned dynamics, a case study of the city water fluoridation programs will be used. The case of the city water fluoridation programs is appropriate for the following reasons:

First, while it relates to a public health issue that requires a thorough understanding of complex scientific evidence related to the safety and potential harms of fluorine, the final decision ultimately exerts significant and direct influence on the everyday life of residents', thus it serves as a critical issue for the residents themselves.

Second, the long history of the program allows us to grasp historical changes in the methods and intensity of citizen participation in local government decision-making. Since its adoption in the early 1980s, the program has been in place for almost 30 years. This was a period of time when Korea experienced numerous political and social changes, therefore we can observe changes in attitudes as well as role changes of various participants, including the local governments and assemblies, citizen groups, oral health experts, and ordinary local residents.

The methods that were used in this study were as follows. First, government reports, news clips, and materials from environmental groups were examined. Second, telephone interviews were conducted with 26 civil servants working at twenty water purification plants. The first series of phone interviews were conducted in November, 2005, and complementary interviews were added in March, 2006 and July, 2008. Third, telephone interviews were conducted in July, 2008, with two people from a citizen group that was heavily involved in the city water fluoridation program.

Theoretical Perspectives

Argument 1: Is Citizen Participation Always Good?

In general, the term 'citizen participation' implies a consecutive process in which residents are provided with information and take part in the process of decision-making (Lee, 2002). As for the definition of citizen participation, a diverse range of definitions have been proposed. Verba and Nie described it as ordinary citizens' activities which are intended to exercise influence on public plans and policies (Verba and Nie, 1972). More broadly, Barnes and Kaase (1979) defined citizen participation as political activities by citizens to influence governmental plans and activities, not only through legitimate methods such as voting, but also through public protests and violence.

Despite the diverse definitions, several common points characterize citizen participation (Lee, 1993). First, citizen participation is different from that of political experts, as it represents the amateur activity of ordinary citizens. Second, the goal of citizens' activities is to exert meaningful influence upon public issues. Third, participation does not end with the citizens' mere recognition of pending issues or attitude changes on certain topics, but rather it involves specific actions and activities. Fourth, activities that support government decisions are also considered as one type of participation.

Citizen participation is now considered to be the most important component of local governance, as the government at a local level is required to be more responsive to citizen's desires and needs to be more effective in service delivery by building a participation mechanism and becoming more accountable to its citizens (Choi, 1990). Zimmerman points out the importance of citizen participation in local governance through the following four aspects (Zimmerman, 1986: 2–4). First, citizen participation enhances the capability of local governments, specifically related to identification and solution of problems. Second, as local residents' immediate knowledge and experiences with local situations and problems increase through participation, the decision-making processes of local governments often improves as well. Third, by sharing responsibilities and accountabilities with local residents, implementation becomes more effective. Finally, local residents' abilities to evaluate policy results improve as residents are provided with more information. They can judge the activities and achievements of the local government from a more professional standpoint. In addition, citizen participation in local governance may bring efficiency gains in local decision making simply by exposing policy-makers to the preferences and political demands of residents. Citizen participation systems, such as referenda, resident proposals and resident recalls, often arbitrate and solve conflicts that could occur between different agencies of the local governments.

At the same time, Zimmerman points out concerns over the potential negative effects that could occur with increasing citizen participation (Zimmerman, 1986). First, decision-making via citizen participation can be expensive due to additional expenses related to providing information to citizens, holding public hearings, and executing referenda. Second, citizen participation can delay the decision-making process. Third, lay citizens often do not possess the competence necessary to make adequate judgments with respect to the technical aspects of the pending issues. Fourth, if residents seek their own interests over the common good of society at large, conflicts may be triggered among residents in different regions. Fifth, representativeness of participants may be questioned. Sixth, there may be a value conflict if participants hold substantially different values from those held by a majority of elected officers and bureaucrats.

Argument 2: Is Citizen Participation Good for Scientific Issues?

Advocates of citizen participation argue that even in the decision-making process of health and environmental issues that are often considered much too technical and scientific for ordinary people to grasp, citizen participation is becoming more important. They say that citizens' roles are changing—from passive ones, where the public simply conforms to the final decisions made by experts and policy-makers, to more assertive ones, where residents themselves search for information or political measures and exercise their political rights (Baram, 1973; Ben-Dor, 1975; Fiorino, 1990; Frankenfeld, 1992; Sclove, 1998; Foltz, 1999; Kho, 2003; Kim, 2005; Lee, 2007). On the other hand, opponents argue that health and environmental policy issues are much too specialized, technical, and scientific for the general populace, so non-professional citizens may misunderstand core problems of the pending issues and stubbornly persist due to their ignorance.

More specifically, opponents of citizen participation in scientific/technology policy decision-making extend their arguments based on either technological determinism or professionalism. Technological determinism indicates that scientific technology or professional knowledge evolves according to its own internal logic, rather than by changes in society. According to them, developments in technology have a unidirectional influence on society, and not vice versa (Bimber, 1990). Humans may not decide the direction of science and technology development through aggressive selection or intervention and consequently they believe that it is the new forms of science and technology development that exercise influence upon society. From the perspective of technological determinism, citizen participation in choosing technology is, in principle, neither possible nor recommendable, because the direction of technical development is, in a way, predetermined.

Arguments based on professionalism extend the same conclusion based on different rationales. They object to the idea of citizen participation in decision-making related to science and technological issues, assuming that only the experts, who are specially trained to cope with scientific and technical matters, are qualified and capable of making decisions in those areas. To them, characteristics of science and technology are much too complicated and complex for ordinary people to understand. According to this position, ordinary citizens lack qualifications or necessary abilities to take a meaningful part in the scientific and technical decision-making process. Also, citizens are accused of easily becoming inappropriately emotional and irrational.

On the other hand, there are contentions that support the necessity and importance of citizen participation in scientific and technological issues. Arguments that say citizen participation is required and available for scientific and technical policy decision-making are as follows. First, scientific technology itself is often socially formed (Bijker, Hughes and Pinch, 1987; Bijker and Law, 1992). Second, scientific technologies also have fundamentally public characteristics (Elliott and Elliott, 1976; Foltz, 1999; Dahl, 1985). Third, lay knowledge accumulated in the lives of ordinary citizens can represent critical components of developments in science and technology (Wynne, 1991). Finally, accountability and effectiveness are important components of all public decision-making and should be pursued at the same time (Brooks, 1984). Lastly citizen participation can promote accountability and effectiveness.

In Western society, since the 1960s, there has been increasing recognition that scientific and technical policies have social and political aspects. Accordingly, participation of ordinary citizens in scientific and technical policies has been developed in diverse patterns (Jasanoff and Markle, 1995). Especially in the United States, diverse models of citizen participation have been developed and experimented with for the last 30 years.

Dynamics of Citizen Participation in Policy Making

Models of Citizen Participation

Citizen participation in the governmental policy decision-making processes can appear in various forms. For example, in European countries, models of citizen participation in policy decision-making have developed in many different patterns, varying from passive ones to more assertive ones, from non-official to official participation, and from indirect to direct forms. Lee (1993) classifies forms of citizen participation based on the following four criteria: 1) the degree of systematization, customization, and lawfulness, 2) the degree of activeness and spontaneity, 3) the participating stage, and 4) collectivity. Arnstein (1971: 217–218) has categorized them into 8 levels in a ladder pattern from the lowest to the highest level according to how much influence citizen participation exerts upon the final decisions. In the model, the first stage of 'manipulation' and the second stage of 'therapy' contain non-participation characteristics. In these two stages, citizens do not participate in designing and executing programs, but are treated as subjects for 'education' and 'cure'. The third stage of 'information', the 4th stage of 'consultation', and the 5th stage of 'placation' all contain features of tokenism, and in these stages citizens are allowed to express their own opinions and are listened to. However, citizens still do not have the 'muscle' to exert any real power on decision-making. The 6th stage of 'partnership', the 7th stage of 'delegating power', and the 8th stage of 'citizen control' finally begin to exhibit some characteristics of genuine citizen power. In these stages, citizens obtain a major position of decision-making or all-inclusive power.

Zimmerman (1986: 6–13) has categorized participation models into active and passive forms based on the level of participants' spontaneity. The passive forms include public relations, information provision, and opinion surveys. These are examples of cases where public officials provide citizens with information on pending issues. Sometimes, government officials even manipulate public opinions regarding pending problems. Active forms of participation include town meetings, public hearings, citizen advisory committees, city councils, referenda, resident initiatives, resident recall, and volunteer activity. Yoo (2003) classified the models of citizen participation into three types: 'administrative mobilization,' 'collaborative cooperation,' and 'autogeneous organization'. Chun, et al. (2003) classified the models into 'institutional' and the 'non-institutional' citizen participation. 'Institutional participation,' includes election/voting, neighborhood meetings, public hearings, petitions, resident audit claims, committees, and ordinance establishment, etc. 'Non-institutional' forms include interviews with a local government head, petition through a local council, interviews with local officials in charge, group civil petitions, and demonstrations. Among the diverse citizen participation models, typical models used in actual policy decision-making processes are referenda, public hearings, opinion surveys, negotiation on regulations, collegiums, civil jury/citizen panels, citizen advisory committees and focus groups (Lee, 2002). A short description of each of the characteristic types is shown in Table 1.

Table 1. Typical Models of Citizen Participation

Participation Model		Characteristics of Participants	Required Time	Special Feature /Mechanism
Passive Partic-ipation	Opinion Survey	• Quick surveys using a large-size sampling over diverse areas.	• One-time phone survey can take 5–7 days	• Conducted through phone or face-to-face interviews • Can include multiple questions • Useful for collection of residents' knowledge and attitudes • Results can vary by sample or questionnaire wording
	Refer-endum	• Total population of a country or a small area may participate.	• Only time for planning, public announcement and implementation is required. • Before the referendum, public hearing and public announcements may be useful	• Asking voters to make one choice among alternative options • Each participant has identical influence and the final result has politically binding force.
Active Partic-ipation	Public Hearing	• Only interested citizens participate. • The number of participants may be limited by space. • Participation may be limited to experts or politicians.	• It may take several weeks or years.	• If a public hearing is held during weekdays, participation may be limited. • Citizens may express their opinions, but cannot directly influence the results.
	Negoti-ation on Regula-tion	• Only a small number of people representing interested parties may participate. • Allows citizen representatives to participate.	• Sometimes necessary to set up a time limit in advance • It usually takes 4~8 months.	• Negotiation between representatives of interested party and hosting agency at the negotiation committee • Reach a consensus about specific problems are necessary

Participation Model		Characteristics of Participants	Required Time	Special Feature / Mechanism
	Colle-gium	• Possible to represent ordinary citizens to the some extent. • Selecting 10–16 volunteers who have no prior prejudice against the pending issues.	• It is necessary to give prior explanation and lectures in order to provide citizen panels with information related to the subject. • It takes about 3 days for a general meeting.	• Questions prepared by citizen panels are presented to experts. • Open meeting. Results for core questions will be announced through press conference.
Active Partic-ipation	Civil Jury	• Composed of 12–24 ordinary citizens selected at random by an independent institution.	• Preparation can take 3–4 months, and the session lasts for 4–5 days in general.	• The process is composed of setting up problems, selection of jury members, discussion, announcement of policy advice, and self evaluation
	Citizen advisory commit-tee	• A group of 20–25 citizens is organized at random to represent diverse groups and communities.	• Preparation can take a couple of months • Sessions may require 4–5 days.	• The goal is to provide citizens' comments on the issues in debates. • Because the meetings may be held several times on an issue, the total number of participants may be several hundred.
	Focus Group	• A small group discussion composed of 5–8 people who represent residents. • Can be conducted with multiple groups.	• Usually a 2-hour meeting can be held once or repeated several times.	• conducted as free discussion or one with a prepared scenario • Useful for listening to opinions and understanding knowledge of citizens through discussion at a group situation.

Sources: Lee's table (2002: 29–30) modified.

Expansion of City Water Fluoridation Programs in Korea

City water fluoridation programs came into operation in Korea in the following order. In the late 1970s, when the Ministry of Health and Social Affairs learned that fluoridation of municipal water was a very effective, efficient, and economic tool to promote the oral health of residents, it established a specific plan for implementation. Water supply fluoridation plans were first implemented in two cities, Jinhae City (1981. 4) and Cheong-ju City (1982. 2), as demonstration projects. In this process, the government had consulted the Korean Oral Health Association (Kim, 1987). It is notable that international trends, such as the WHO and the United States policy efforts, at the time also influenced this initiative in Korea. The city water fluoridation program was adopted as an important part of the public oral health program of the WHO in the year of 1970. The West Pacific Subdivision of the WHO strongly recommended that Korea implement fluoridation programs (Suh, 2004). As of March 2006, the fluoridation program in Korea was implemented at 43 water purification plants (about 8%) out of the 540 plants across the country.

Since the late 1990s however, expansion of the operation slowed down with an increasing number of opposing views and claims developing regarding the fluoridation program. Potential harm to one's body and the environment, as well as violations of residents' right to choose, became politically controversial issues. Finally, 13 purification plants, including those in the 2 cities of Cheongju and Gwacheon decided to stop the fluoridation program.

In summary, 39 local governments (about 12%) among 234 districts (Ministry of Government and Home Affairs, 2006: 392) implemented the water fluoridation program. When classified by initial dates of operation, 3 plants in the 1980s, 25 plants in the 1990s, and 15 plants in the 2000s began fluoridation, and the program was fully implemented in the late 1990s. There is a 10-year interval between the demonstration projects in Jinhae and Cheongju City and the water fluoridation program in Gwacheon City.

The following factors were the major forces for rapid expansion of water fluoridation implementation in the late 1990s. First, the establishment of the National Health Promotion Law stipulated that the fluoridation program was to become a mandatory program by law (established on January 1st, 1995; Law No. 4914). Second, as the Ministry of Health and Social Affairs selected the water fluoridation program as a major public health initiative for 25 areas nation-wide in December 1997, the Korean government allocated a separate budget which was specified for the program. Third, evaluation studies of the demonstration projects showed significant positive effects on prevention of dental caries.

The Administrative and Legal Grounds of the Program

In order to understand the dynamics between the local governments and citizen participation, it is necessary to understand the local administrative system and legal grounds of the program. The initial legal grounds for the water fluoridation program can be attributed to the National Health Promotion Law (established on January 1st, 1995; Law No. 4914). Under this law, the decision power for implementation of the water fluoridation program resided with the central and local governments. There were no mandatory regulations that required the collection of local residents' opinions.

Next, the 'Oral Health Law' was legislated in 2000 (Law No. 6163), and the power for decisions related to the water fluoridation program implementation were transferred to the local entities—to the local governors, mayors, county governors, district chiefs, or the Korea Water Resources Cooperation. This is an important detail related to the history of decentralization and citizen participation in Korea, because collection of local residents' opinions when it comes to implementation decisions became mandatory; the law clarified that the decision-making process for the water fluoridation program implementation shall include an active collection of local resident's opinions and the final decision shall be made based on the result. This means that the decision power for the water fluoridation program implementation was partially transferred to the hands of local residents. It should be noted that the Ministry of Health and Social Affairs had consistently held fast to a supporting position since the demonstration projects of the water fluoridation program in 1981. Therefore, changes in the local councils and the opinion of local residents, as well as citizens' groups positions, were the main forces exerting significant influence upon the decisions.

What is interesting is that water fluoridation programs are administered and implemented by two institutions: the public health centers and the water supply and drainage stations. The public health centers are in charge of planning the water fluoridation program, compiling the necessary budget, and collecting residents' opinions. The water supply and drainage stations take care of maintenance and management of machinery facilities, and were responsible for adding the proper amount of fluorine to the water system. There are potential conflicts between the institutions, as the two institutions operate on different legal grounds. The public health centers work based on the 'Oral Health Law', while the water supply and drainage stations operate according to the 'Water Supply Act', Cooperation between the two systems is critical for smooth implementation of the water fluoridation. A simplified flow chart of the administrative system and the legal grounds for the water fluoridation is shown in Figure 1.

Figure 1. Administrative System and Legal Grounds of the Water Fluoridation Program

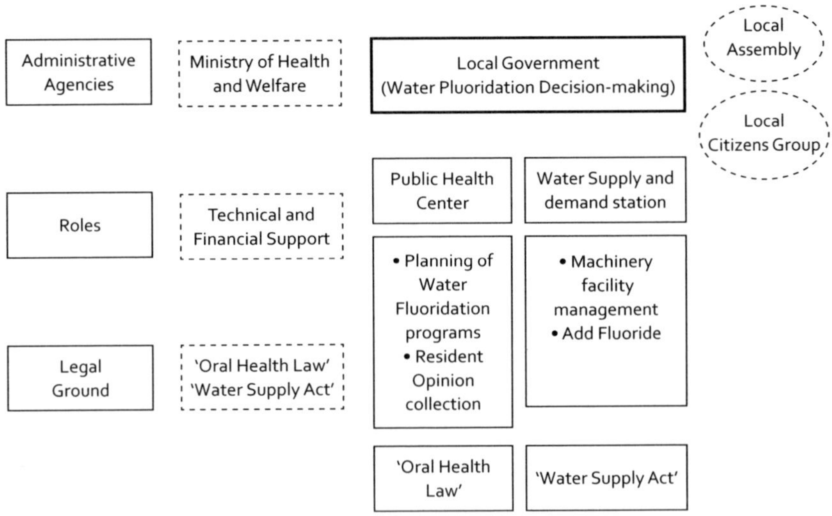

Citizen Participation in Implementing the Programs

With the announcement of the positive effects of the water fluoridation program on dental caries prevention in Jinhae and Cheongju City, local demands for water fluoridation rose sharply and voluntary civil efforts to adopt the policy decision also increased. First of all, the Korean Dental Association submitted petitions for the program's implementation to local governments in cooperation with citizen groups. The association distributed public relations materials to inform residents of the positive effects of water fluoridation. The citizen groups in each area placed placards, prepared parades and campaigns in cooperation with each other in order to urge local governments to implement the program. The local governments then sent official documents to the central government to secure the budget for facility construction. At the same time, the residents' opinions were collected through public hearings and opinion surveys (From an interview with the City Water Fluoridation Program Technology Support Team, 2001).

The participation models which were developed during the implementation and decision-making process of the water fluoridation programs can be roughly divided into the following five types (See Table 3 and 4). First, a non-participation model, in which decisions were made under the leadership of the local government without residents' participation; second, opinion surveys of local residents were conducted; third, public hearings and open forums were organized; fourth, citizen participation by means of field trips, petitions or proclamations was cultivated; and fifth, referenda were held for the first time in Korea on the topic of the water fluoridation program's implementation. Cases of resident non-participation models are presented in Table 3.

Examples of non-participation decisions are Jinahe City and Cheongju City—the first two 'fluoride program showcase' projects in Korea. The non-participating models can be divided into 3 patterns based on the leading entity of decision-making. First, Jinhae (1 purification plant) and Cheongju (3 purification plants) are cases where the decision was made under the leadership of the central government. The implementation decisions were made in the early 1980s before the local governance system was introduced, and the central government made decisions after a series of consultations with public health experts. In such an undemocratic political environment of society in Korea at that time, non-participation in decision-making was common. The following comment from a government official confirms this view.

"Back then, resident opinions were rarely collected in imple-

Table 3. Places with Non-Participation in the Implementation Decision-making of the Water Fluoridation Programs in Korea

Participation Model	Leadership Entity	Operation Area	Name of Purification Plant	Initial Date of Operation
Non-Participation	Central Government	Jinhae City	Seokdong Purification Plant	1981.4
	Local government or Local Assembly	Cheongju City	Cheongju, Youngwoon, Jibuk Purification Plant	1997,1982,1982
		Yeongwol County	Yeongwol Purification Plant	2002.12
		Gumi City	Gumi Broad Range Purification Plant	1999.2
		Changnyeong County	Sangwol Purification Plant	2000.1
	Experts*	Namyangju City	Whado Purification Plant	2000.11
		Yeoncheon County	Yeoncheon Purification Plant	1999.8
		Namhae County	Asan Purification Plant	1999.1

* 'Experts' means oral health experts from the public health centers, the Korean Dental Association, dental professionals, and others.

Sources: Drawn up on the basis of home page database of the City water fluoridation program technology support team (2001), Korea Oral Health Association, and phone interviews shown in the Table 2.

menting a new program. The concept of citizen participation in our administration became important only after the democratic election system was set up (From an Interview with a government official, 2005. 11)."

Second are the cases where local governments or the local councils made decisions. Decisions in Yeongwol County (1 purification plant), Gumi City (1 purification plant) and Changnyeong County fall into this pattern. These are cases where winning an election itself was regarded as collection of resident opinions, because implementing the fluoridation program was announced as an election pledge of the candidates for mayors or county governors during the local election process.

The final types are those where the decision-making of the program was led by oral health experts from the public health centers and dental associations, as well as dental health professionals. Yeoncheon County and Namhae County fall into this pattern. At that time, resident opinion collection was not legislatively mandatory. In Namyangju City, the decision related to implementation was made without conducting a resident opinion collection, as the other purification plant in the same administrative district had already implemented the water fluoridation program.

Citizen participation cases are presented in the Table 4. As shown in the table, there were 22 purification plants where the public-opinion surveys were implemented under the leadership of oral health experts, local citizen groups, the local governments, and local assemblies. The results show that public-opinion polls were the most common form of citizen participation. It is especially notable that resident opinion surveys were conducted at 14 of the 22 purification plants, even when the opinion survey was not defined as a legislative mandate.

Next, there are other citizen participation models, such as public hearings, open forums and explanation meetings. As shown in Table 4, these models were used in implementing water fluoridation programs in Hampyeong, Chilgok, Cheongyang, and Hapcheon Counties. Frequently, these methods were used in combination with opinion surveys or petitions to other local autonomous entities or local assemblies (e.g., Daejeon Metro City, Namyangju City, Asan and Jinju City). Third, field trips to a plant with the fluoridation programs, or visiting local entities and assemblies to make petitions, were other methods of participation. These were

Table 4. Citizen Participation in Implementation of the Fluoridation Programs in Korea

Participation Model	Entity of Leadership	Operation Area	Name of Purification Plant
Opinion Survey	Experts	Namyangju City	Dogok purification plant
		Gwangju City	Gwangju purification plant 1, 2
		Okcheon County	Okcheon purification plant
		Gyeongju City	Bomun purification plant, Tapdong purification plant
		Gimhae City	Samgye purification plant 1, 2
	Local Citizen Groups	Gwacheon City	Gwacheon purification plant
		Yeosu City	Hakyong purification plant
	Local autonomous entity or Local assembly	Daejeon Metro City	Songchon purification plant
		Ansan City	Ansan, Yeonseong and Banwol purification plant
		Euiwang City	Cheonggye purification plant
		Anseong City	Anseong purification plant
		Asan City	Yongwha purification plant
		Seosan City	Suseok purification plant
		Pohang City	Yukang, Yangdeok purification plant
		Gurye County	Gurye purification plant
		Jinju City	Purification plant 1, 2
		North Jeju County	Hanlim purification plant
Public Hearing Open forum	Experts	Woolsan Metro City	Hoiya purification plant 1, 2
		Hampyeong County	Hampyeong purification plant
		Chilgok County	Industrial complex purification plant
	Local Citizen Groups	Daejeon Metro City	Songchon purification plant
		Ulsan Metro City	Hoiya purification plant 1, 2
	Local entity or Local assembly	Namyangju City	Dogok purification plant,
		Kangneung City	Yeongok purification plant
		Asan City	Yongwha purification plant
		Cheongyang	Cheongyang purification plant
		Jinju City	Purification plant 1, 2
		Hapcheon County	Hapcheon purification plant
Others (Field trips, Petition to local government and assembly, Public statement, etc.)	Daejeon Metro City, Ulsan Metro City, Asan City, etc.		
Referendum	No case was found		

Sources: The same as the Table 3.

also used in conjunction with opinion surveys, public hearings, and open forums. Examples include cases in Daejeon Metropolitan City and Asan City. Finally, there was a referendum which is frequently used in foreign countries but was not used in Korea for water fluoridation decisions (Kang et al., 2005: 58–9).

Characteristics of citizen participation in implementing the water fluoridation programs in Korea can be summarized as follows: First, opinion surveys appeared to be the most common mode of citizen participation. This indicates that, according to Zimmerman's typology (1986: 6–13), a passive form of participation was preferred. This tells us that citizen participation in the decision-making process of water fluoridation in Korea is not yet active, and the means of participation are still limited. Thus there still is ample room for further efforts to utilize diverse models that allow more active forms of participation.

Second, the introduction of local governance systems played a catalytic role and helped open a door to citizen participation in the implementation of the water fluoridation programs. Before 1995, we see very few cases of citizen participation in decision-making with respect to the water fluoridation program. However, after the formation of local governments, we observed a number of opinion surveys conducted even before they became legislatively mandated. This may constitute strong support for the theory that the introduction of local governance is closely connected to flourishing citizen participation (Zimmerman, 1986; Lee, 1993).

Third, oral health experts, local citizen groups, the central or local government, or the local assembly were the main participants who were intensely involved in the decision-making process with regard to fluoridation programs and who promoted citizen participation.

Citizen Participation in Suspending the Decision of the Program

As of 2006, 13 purification plants (about 30%) in 10 local governments, including Cheongju and Gwacheon City, stopped their water fluoridation programs after the initial implementation (Table 5). The suspension decisions were primarily made during the period of 2003 and 2004. Citizen participation in making the suspension decisions is characterized as follows. First, in some places, the local assembly or local government, due to intense opposition by local citizen groups, made suspension decisions. There were signature campaigns, interviews with local governments and assemblies, petitions, and street demonstrations, as well as the distribution of materials with opposing views and arguments. Five cases fall into this category. Sometimes, the local assembly cancelled the budget which had already been allocated for the program (Daejeon Metro City (1), Gwacheon City (1), Gyeongju City (2)). In one particular case, the local government made a decision to delay implementation of the program (Geochang County (1)). A common feature among these cases is that the local governments did not conduct public opinion surveys before they made such decisions. They made the suspension decision based on intense opposition activities of citizens groups.

Second, there were cases in which opinion surveys were conducted before making suspension decisions. In the City of Chungjoo, public opinion surveys were conducted and the suspension decision was made based on the results of the public opinion surveys. Interestingly, we found that the city's decision to suspend the program was also heavily affected by the strong opposition of citizen groups after all (from interviews with local government officials and a member of a citizen group, 2008. 7). After the 'Citizen Action for Suspension of Cheongju City Water Fluoridation' was

Table 5. Citizen Participation Models in Making Suspension Decision of the Fluoridation Programs

Local Governments		Suspended Purification Plant	Background of Suspension Decision-making and Citizen Participation Model
Daejeon Metro City (1)	All area of Dung-gu, Part of Jung-gu and Daedeok-gu	Songchon Purification Plant	• Operation expense curtailed by the local assembly • Citizen groups visited the city hall and the local assembly to express opposing opinions • Resident opinion survey was not performed.
Gyeonggi Province (3)	Gwancheon City	Gwacheon Purification Plant	• Budget curtailed by the local assembly due to opposition by citizen groups. • Resident opinion survey was not performed.
	Namyangju City	Dogok Purification Plant	• Suspended temporarily due to construction.
		Whado Purification Plant	• Suspension decision made by the local government. • Resident opinion survey was not performed.
	Euiwang City	Cheonggye Purification Plant	• Suspended by the local government due to the accidental leakage of fluorine into the Hakeui stream in December 2002.
Chungcheongbuk Province (3)	Heungdeok-gu Cheongju City	Cheongju Purification Plant (Korea Water Resources Cooperation Daecheong Dam)	• Suspension decisions were made after discussion with the local government (Cheongju City residents' opinion survey results were reflected in the final decision).
	Sangdang-gu Cheongju City	Youngwoon Purification Plant	• Opposition to the program prevailed in the resident opinion survey.
	Sangdang-gu Cheongju City	Jibuk Purification Plant	• Same as above.
Gyeondsangbuk Province (4)	Pohang City(Nam-gu)	Youkang Purification Plant	• City assembly cut the budget despite no differences in the result of opinion survey.
	Pohang City (Buk-gu)	Yangdeok Purification Plant	• Same as above.
	Gyeongju City	Bomun Purification Plant	• Budget curtailed by the local assembly due to opposition of citizen groups. • Resident opinion survey was not performed.
		Tapdong Purification Plant	• Same as above.
Gyeongsangnam Province (1)	Geochang County	Geochang Purification Plant	• Even after the completion of construction, the program was not implemented by the local government due to the opposition of citizen groups.

* The number in parentheses refers to the number of purification plants in the area.
Sources: Same as the Table 3.

established in December 2001, debates regarding the safety issues and accountability of the fluoridation programs were intensified. The 'Citizen Action' group utilized diverse activities such as one-person rallies, demonstration rallies in front of the city hall, citizen campaigns and signature events, petitions to the Chunbuk Province and Cheongju City, and the publishing of pamphlets with the title "Stop the Water Fluoridation!" Finally, in December 2002, the Cheongju City Assembly yielded to citizen groups' demands and decided to cancel the 2003 budget allocations for this program. At the same time, they announced that the municipal government would make the final decision based on the results of the public opinion surveys. In November 2003, a survey with 1,000 Cheongju citizens was conducted. Opposition prevailed by a margin of 38 votes (452 votes in favor and 490 dissenting votes) and the fluoridation program was suspended by December 31, 2003. One thing to note here is that in Chungjoo, there was an agreement made in advance on how to make the final decision, i.e., based on the results of the public opinion survey.

It is notable however, that in some places, the results of the surveys were not used in making the final suspension decisions. For example, Pohang City (with two purification plants) is a case in which the opinion survey was conducted, but the result was not used in making the final decision.

> "Pohang City authority implemented the resident opinion survey on whether to continue the program or not to resolve the conflicts between the supporting and opposing views on water fluoridation. However, the public opinion survey results were not utilized in making the final decision. The proportions of supporting responses and opposing ones turned out to be very close. The votes in favor occupied 41.2 percent, while the opposition was 41.1 percent. The program was

> finally suspended when the local assembly decided to cancel the program's budget for good (from an interview with a local official, 2005. 11)."

According to the local government official we interviewed, the result of the opinion surveys showed no differences, the city had to make the final decision based on the opinions of professional institutions, public hearings, results of the questionnaire survey, and the collection of council members' opinions (Pohang City Assembly, Minute of the 89th General Meeting).

Third, there were cases where the water fluoridation program was suspended due to the different stances of the public health center and the water supply and drainage station. In this case, the water supply and drainage station stopped adding fluorine into the city water first, and subsequently the local government followed and made the suspension decision. Public opinion surveys were not conducted. In this case, there were no significant activities by opposing citizen groups, nor ordinary citizens, unlike other cases related to the suspension decision (based on interviews with 2 local government officials, 2008. 7).

A government official from the water supply and drainage station describes the situation as the following:

> "In the beginning, there was a procedural problem in the implementation decision-making process. The programs started without conducting an opinion survey as required by law. Our work is based on the 'Water Supply Act', not the 'Oral Health Law'. According to the 'Water Supply Act', there is no basis for adding fluorine. I consider that the water fluoridation program is a kind of medical treatment for the public. If the program is implemented without going through the process of opinion surveys, there is a risk that residents who do not

> want fluorine in their drinking water may initiate a civil suit. We were aware of intense opposition to water fluoridation program in the other regions so, we decided to suspend the program temporarily (2005. 11) Until we got the results of the resident opinion survey (from an interview with the station official, 2008. 7)."

On the other hand, an official of the public health center who was in charge of the opinion survey stated the following.

> "We regard the water fluoridation program as a good public health effort which provides stable and significant benefits to the public. We believed that the program should continue. At that time, we actually set up a plan to conduct an opinion survey with a professional research institution in order to guarantee objectiveness of the results. However, the chief of our institution did not approve the idea, so the plan was dropped. Looking back at it now, I think that the temporary suspension was merely an excuse by the water supply and drainage station which wanted to suspend the water fluoridation program in order to avoid any potential blame. It now seems that the chief was on the side of the water supply and drainage station (From an interview with a local official from the public health center, 2008. 7)."

In this case, the procedural issues that the water supply and drainage station raised were an excuse for them to avoid any political troubles. After all, the suspension decision was made due to conflicts between institutions that had different political views.

Fourth, there were cases where the fluoridation program was suspended due to problems with operating the purification plants. In the purification plant of Namyangju City, the program was suspended during reconstruction. The purification plant of another city in the Gyeonggi Province also falls into this category. In this case, the suspension of the program was caused by accidental leakage of fluorine which resulted in excessive amounts of fluorine in local tap water. No resident opinion surveys were conducted regarding re-starting the program later on.

In sum, suspension decisions were made in many different ways. There were cases in which the local assembly cut the program budget when it faced strong opposition by local citizen groups. Sometimes, the local government suspended the program on its own. In some places, the decision was made based on the results of public opinion surveys. In addition, there were cases where the program was suspended due to problems in operating the purification plant. As in the case of implementation decisions, no case of using referenda when making the suspension decisions was found. It is also worth noting that, when compared to the implementation decision-making of the water fluoridation program where various actors, including the local government, oral health experts, and citizen groups were involved, the main driver of the suspension decision was strong opposition raised by citizen groups.

We found that the results of opinion surveys were not always used in making the final decision. Except in Cheongju City, where the method of deciding whether or not to suspend the program was agreed upon in advance to be public opinion surveys, results of the public opinion surveys were not always utilized (as specified by law). While the public opinion surveys had more influence on implementation decisions, we often observe that this was not so when making the decision to suspend the program. This suggests that agreements, made in advance among the policy makers, regarding how to make final decisions and what role citizen participation will take in the process of local policy decision-making, is of significant importance. Finally, there was a case where a disagreement among institutions, such as between the local government agency and the local assembly, or between the public health centers and the water supply and drainage station, caused the suspension of the program.

Conclusion

Since the introduction of the decentralization reforms in the 1990s, opportunities for citizen participation in local policy making processes, such as city planning, site selection for nuclear waste disposal facilities, and administrative district amendments, have been expanded. The number of cases, in which policies are accepted, refused, or delayed by citizen participation during the process of policy decision-making, is rapidly increasing (Baram, 1973; Fiorino, 1990; Lee, 1993, 1997; Jung, 2000; Yoo, 2001; Kim et al., 2002; Song, 2003; Yoo, 2003; Chun et al., 2003; Choi and Lee, 2005).

This development of citizen participation thus enhances political development. In this chapter, we looked at the role of citizen participation in local policy making based on the case of the water fluoridation program. Several interesting features stand out.

First, since the introduction of the local governance system, the desire for participation of local citizen groups and residents in local health policy decision-making was significantly heightened. At the same time, it made the local governments and the local councils more sensitive to pressures from citizen groups and the public. Local governments appeared to be sensitively responding to opposing opinions. Such tendencies were clearly shown, as we found that a number of programs were suspended with opposing activities in the neighboring areas, even though there was no visible opposition activity in the pertinent area. As a result, the size of the population affected by the program was continuously reduced, from 10.5 percent in 2001 to 7.8 percent in 2004 (Jung et al., 2005).

This is intriguing, as we know that the fluoridation program was promoted as one of the most important public health programs by the central government. This implies that after the adoption of the local governance system, promoting a local policy for the central government became harder when compared to the time before the structural changes in governance system. As we also observed in the cases of selecting the radioactive waste disposal sites, or establishing for-profit hospitals in Jeju Province, in order for the local policy agenda of the central government to be successfully promoted, stronger initiatives and well-planned strategies seem to be required.

Second, while it seems that the introduction of a local governance system has expanded the opportunities for citizen participation in local policy decision-making, in reality, citizen participation seems to remain at a superficial level. Citizen participation in making the fluoridation decision is now guaranteed by law, but we found that in reality a considerable number of local governments use citizen participation according to their own convenience. In the case of water fluoridation, citizen participation itself was not seriously taken into account in making the implementation decision until the early 1990s. Since the mid 1990s, citizen participation has increased, but was limited in scope. Despite the nominal increase, the window of opportunity for genuine participation has been very limited, and most of them have been in the form of a passive approach. For instance, public opinion surveys were inevitably implemented, but only after significant conflicts were raised over the water fluoridation program.

Third, regardless of whom the leading entity of policy decision making was, both in implementation decisions or suspension decisions, a limited number of forms of citizen participation, such as opinion surveys, public hearings, or open forums, were used. In comparison to Western Europe where citizen participation flourished from the early 1990s, in Korea, citizen participation in the local policy decision-making process has not yet been very well developed. The citizen participation models which are most frequently used at the governmental level in Korea are public hearings and advisory committees. Public hearings are now considered a routine process to go through before making final decisions. However, most public hearings are regarded as a rite of passage when obtaining procedural accountability, rather than serving as a real outlet for citizen participation where opinions of residents are reflected in policies. As for advisory committees, while more frequently used since the late 1990s, they only take the role of providing advice and do not have much compelling power (Lee, 2002).

Fourth, we found that even in cases where public opinion surveys were conducted and their results were reflected in the final decision-making, the survey was mostly conducted only on a one-time basis. Among the areas where a suspension decision was made, we did not observe a case where a local government conducted public opinion surveys about re-operation of the program. In other words, once a suspension decision was made, the decision remains for years afterwards without additional surveys. Considering that the residents' degree of knowledge regarding a policy as well as their attitudes toward a policy can change dramatically in response to new information and conditions (Kang et al., 2005; Kang et al., 2007), we cannot say that such a practice faithfully reflects true citizen participation. It also shows that the goal of making the local governance system a truly democratic system with meaningful citizen participation has not yet been achieved in Korea.

In sum, on a positive side, we can say that the introduction of the local governance system has nevertheless expanded the opportunities of citizen participation in local health policy decision making, and there were a number of cases in which the decision to implement or suspend the water fluoridation program was affected by residents' opinions or citizen groups. Based on this trend, we may be able to predict that the influence of citizen participation will grow.

This also means that to realize more advanced local governance in the future, more aggressive and active methods of citizen participation are necessary, instead of the negative and passive modes of participation that are common now. A good example of meaningful and persistent citizen participation is Jinhae City, where the water fluoridation program was implemented first in Korea. The fluoridation program is still continued and the public opinion surveys are conducted on a regular basis with school parents every 2 years.

Along with this, participation models in more diverse modes which can promote participation of residents from diverse classes and areas should be developed and used. Under such efforts, models should be developed that are appropriate for Korean political circumstances. Old ways are only sufficient in terms of satisfying procedural justice. Only creative and aggressive attempts that defy existing ways of thinking will nurture future development in Korean democracy.

A fundamental question about the scientific truth remains. Unless the true effects of fluorine to human body is proved, nobody can tell that the increased citizen participation leading to decrease the programs in Korea might be good for citizen's health.

If decentralization needs to accompany the quality of life with economic growth, scholars should think about what the ideal model of participation under the constraints of scientific uncertainty is.

Note

The early version of this study was published in Kim, D. and M., Kang. 2008. Citizen Participation in the Local Public Health Decision Making: The Water Fluoridation Program in South Korea, *The Korean Journal of Local Government Studies* 12(3): 173–94. (In Korean)

References

The Ministry of Government Administration and Home Affairs. 2006. *2006 Ministry of Government Administration and Home Affairs*. (In Korean)

Water Fluoridation Technical Supporting Committee. 2001. The Archive of 20 Years' History of the Water Fluoridation. (In Korean)

An, B. 2002. The NGO's Influential Factor on Policymaking: The Separation Policy of Prescribing and Dispensing Drugs in Korea, *Korean Society and Public Administration* 12(4): 321–37. (In Korean)

Arnstein, S.R. 1969. A ladder of Citizen Participation, *Journal of the American Institute of Planners* 35(4): 216–24.

Baram, M.S. 1973. Technology Assessment and Social Control, *Science, New Series* 180(4085): 465–73.

Barnes, S.H., M., Kaase et al. 1979. *Political Action: Mass Participation in Five Western Democracies*, Beverly Hills: Sage Publications.

Ben-Dor, G. 1975. Institutionalization and Political Development: A Conceptual and Theoretical Analysis, *Comparative Studies in Society and History* 17(13): 309–25.

Bijker, W. and J., Law. eds. 1992. *Shaping Technology, Building Society: Studies in Sociotechnical Change*, Cambridge, MA: The MIT Press.

Bijker, W., T., Hughes and T., Pinch. eds. 1987. *The Social Construction of Technological System*, Cambridge. MA: The MIT Press.

Bimber, B. 1990. Karl Marx and the Three Faces of Technological Determinism, *Social Studies of Science* 20(2): 333–51.

Brooks, H. 1984. The Resolution of Technically Intensive Public Policy Disputes, *Science, Technology & Human Values* 9(1): 39–50.

Cho, S. 2002. Citizens for the Water Fluoridation to Prevent the Tooth Decay, *A Workshop to Organize the National Committee for Water Fluoridation* 98-2 http://www.dental.or.kr. In Korean (accessed on March 22, 2008).

Choi, C. 1990. *The Local Autonomical Institutions*, Seoul: Samyoungsa. (In Korean)

Choi, M. and J., Lee. 2005. Analysis of a Local Government Policy

Executive's Support for Resident's Participation and Innovation: Focus on Recognition, Volition, and System, *Korean Public Administration Review* 39(4): 411–30. (In Korean)

Chun, Y., C., J. and Yi., K. 2003. Local Autonomy of Korea and Citizen Participation, *Korean Journal of Public Administration* 41(2): 53–83. (In Korean)

Dahl, R. 1985. *Controlling Nuclear Weapons: Democracy Versus Guardianship*, Syracuse: Syracuse University Press.

Elliott, D. and R., Elliot. 1976. *The Control of Technology*, London: Wykeham Publications.

Fiorino, D.J. 1990. Citizen Participation and Environmental Risk: A Survey of Institutional Mechanisms, *Science, Technology, & Human Values* 15(2): 226–43.

Foltz, F. 1999. Five Arguments for Increasing Public Participation in Making Science Policy, *Bulletin of Science, Technology & Society* 19(2): 117–27.

Frankenfeld, P.J. 1992. Technological Citizenship: A Normative Framework for Risk Studies, *Science, Technology & Human Values* 17(4): 459–84.

Herson, L.J. and J.M., Bolland. 1990. *The Urban Web: Politics, Policy, and Theory*, Chicago: Nelson-Hall Publishers. http://noF.ter.or.kr. In Korean (accessed on March 17, 2008).

Jasanoff, S. and G.E., Markle. eds. 1995. *Handbook of Science and Technology Studies*, London: Routledge.

Jung, S. et al. 2005. The Progressive Strategy and Planing to Promote the Oral Health in Korea (2006–10), *The Ministry of Health and Welfare/Oral Health Promotion Supporting Committee.* (In Korean)

Jung, Y. 2000. Local Resident's Participation in the Local Governance, *East and West Studies* 12(1): 115–31. (In Korean)

Kaase, Max and M., Alan. 1979. Political Action: A Theoretical Perspective, In *Political Action: Mass Participation in Five Western Democracies*, Beverly Hills: Sage publications. Barnes and Kaase. eds. 27–56.

Kang, M. et al. 2005. Development of a Standard Tool for the Public Opinion Survey on Water Fluoridation, *Management Center for*

Health Promotion. (In Korean)

Kang, M., J., Son and H., Kim. 2005. An Exploratory Application of the Mixed Methods Research: Application of Surveys and Focus Group Interviews for Regional Public Health Issue Decision Making, *Korean Public Administration Review* 41(4): 415–37. (In Korean)

Kho, D. 2003. The Operational Direction of Technology Assessment, *Science & Technology Policy* 143: 2–17. (In Korean)

Kim, C. 2005. Anti-nuclear Movement and the Politics of Local Residents: The Case of Social Movement Against Nuclear Waste Facility in Buan, *Journal Institute Social Research* 6(2): 41–69. (In Korean)

Kim, J. et al. 2007. A Program Evaluation Report on the Outcomes of the Water Fluoridation Program, *Oral Health Promotion Supporting Committee.* (In Korean)

Kim, W. et al. 2002. *Civil Society & Administration*, Seoul: Hyung Seul Publishing. (In Korean)

Kleinman, D.L. 2000. *Science, Technology & Democracy*, Albany: State University of New York Press.

Lee, S. 1993. *Democratic Politics and Citizen's Participation*, Seoul: Samyoungsa. (In Korean)

_______. 1997. Methods to activate citizen participation in local political arena, *Journal of Local Government Studies* 9(2): 1–20. (In Korean)

_______. 2005. *Local Governance*, 2nd. Seoul: Pakyoungsa. (In Korean)

Lee, Y. 2002. Science & Technology Policy and Citizen's Participation Model, *Citizen's Participation in Science, Technology and Environment.* Seoul: Hanul Publishing Company. (In Korean)

_______. 2007. Social Control and Acceptance of Technology: The Politics of Technology Assessment, *Economic & Society Review* 73. (In Korean)

Leiss, W. and Chociolko, C. 1994. *Risk and Responsibility*, McGill-Queen's University Press.

Sclove, R.E. 1998. Better Approaches to Science Policy, *Science* 279(5355): 1283.

Song, K. 2003. Strengthening the Capacity of Local Council and Citizen's participation, *Chung-Ang Public Administration Review* 17(2): 97–118. (In Korean)

Suh, Y. 2004. The Scientific Society and Implantation in Korea: the Water Fluoridation Debate, Presented at the *Korean Association of Science and Technology Studies Conference.* (In Korean)

Verba, S. and H.N., Nie. 1972. *Participation in America: Political Democracy and Social Equality,* New York: Harper and Row.

Wynne, B. 1991. Knowledge in Context, *Science, Technology & Human Values* 19(1): 111–21.

Yoo, H. 2001. A Study on the Methods to Introduce Regional Referendum to Promote Citizen's Participation in the Local Governance, Presented at *The Korean Association for Public Administration Conference.* (In Korean)

Yoo, J. 2003. Methods to Promote Citizen's Participation: on the Perspective of Participatory Democracy, Presented at the *Summer Conference of The Korean Association for Public Administration* 237–54. (In Korean)

Zimmerman, J.F. 1986. *Participatory Democracy: Populism Revisited,* New York: Praeger.

Part IV

Administrative Efficiency

Chapter 8 |

Local Quagos: Their Growth and Accountability with Decentralization

SANG-CHEOUL LEE

Introduction: What is 'Quago'

The trend in public administration since the 1980s has been for governments to move away from using ministries or departments to carry out public tasks in favor of using more autonomous bodies. These bodies include special account budgets, agencies, more autonomous bodies (mabs), state enterprises, local public corporations and commercial organizations. Such trends are related to questions regarding the true size of government, or more particularly governments' tendency to unlimitedly expand.

Quasi-autonomous-non-governmental-organization (Quango) is a more familiar term than quago (quasi-autonomous-governmental organization), but this chapter will make use of the term Quago because we will focus on semi-governmental (departmental) organizations which are more or less under the influence of government. It is all but impossible to find an internationally accepted definition of the term. However it is generally accepted that Quagos fall somewhere between departmental-forms of organization and privatization-forms of organization on the political control continuum. Keeping in mind the following parameters, this chapter will employ the following definition of quago; any organization that spends public money to perform public tasks but has some degree of flexibility regarding the administration of its budget, organizational independence, and autonomy of personnel from the ministry or department that oversees it. The term quago does not refer to a tangible or clear organizational form, but instead refers to a political control continuum on which a range of bodies can be placed (Flinders and Smith, 1999, 4).

This is an interesting concept because it will help us to understand the greyer areas of local governments. Quagos are a ubiquitous feature of the modern public sector throughout the world, with the assertion being made that "If quagos did not exist, they would have to be invented." (Flinders and Smith, 1999, 7). Quagos are not only found in Western countries, but also in the developing world and at the supra-national as well as the sub-national level. This is the phenomenon of 'Quagocratization' according to Pollitt et al.(2003, 13) which means that departmental or ministerial organizations are evolving toward quago-style organizations

In this context, I have chosen the growth of local quagos in Korea as the principal theme of the questions asked in this chapter. The main questions that this chapter deals with are as follows:

First, why have quagos (especially at the local level) become so popular?

This chapter examines in general how the number of quagos has increased significantly and why this expansion has taken place internationally. It also looks at why the number of quagos increased significantly after the Korean local autonomy system was implemented in 1995. The Korean local autonomy system seems to have created momentum for delegating the central government's authority to local governments.

Second, what are the problems created by the rapid growth of quagos' in connection to local political autonomy?

Third, this chapter examines the socio-economic accountability of local quagos in terms of managerial and social efficiency and oversight. It also examines problems and proposes solutions in terms of monitoring quagos to ensure compatibility with democratic control. The recommendations of this chapter focus on under what conditions local quagos perform best.

Theoretical Background of Quagos' Growth

Even though the number of Quagos has increased recently, there is no well established theory which explains the reason for their proliferation. Some theories are applied to particular cases but a general framework which explains their recent popularity is still missing. Pollit et al. (2004) discussed the reason of these agency's growth in the view of three broad epistemological families; the New Institutional Economics (Rational Choice Theory), Traditional Organizational Theory (searching for causes, factors, explanatory variables) and Interpretive/Social Constructivist.

I will focus on the practice of NPM (New Public Management) in relation to the international trend of Quagos' expansion and Social Constructivism which are thus related to the particular phenomena in Korea of Quagos increasing at the lower and upper levels of local autonomous entities. Rational Choice theory, sometimes, is applied successfully in explaining peculiar Korean bureaucratic circumstances in connection with Quagos' growth. Especially because New Public Management emphasizes outsourcing and contracting out in order to increase government's efficiency, it is logical that the use of Quagos will grow.

The traditional bureaucratic structures, which have historically formed the backbone of the state, have begun to crumble at both the national and local levels (Flinders, 1999). It is time for politicians to find new and innovative solutions to public policy utilizing demand flexibility, geographic mobility and administrative decentralization. Consequently traditional governmental organizations are being transformed into quagos.

Advocates of New Public Management (NPM) insist that such bureaucratic structural transformations are helpful to improve the efficiency of management and the responsiveness to customers demands.

In this context, the number of quagos has been consistently increasing internationally. A number of countries (Jamaica, Japan, Tanzania, and the United Kingdom) have launched 'agencification'—transferring as many government activities as possible into new agency-type organizations. In the Netherlands, 40 percent of all quagos were established after 1980. (Pollitt et al., 2001: Pollitt and Talbot, 2004).

Why have quagos become so popular? The main trend of the NPM in Europe has led a transformation of government departments into various types of quagos. One of the main claims of "quagocratization" is that it decreases the number of tasks performed by the central government. Figure 1 and Figure 2 show us a clear comparison of quagocracy and bureaucracy in the Netherlands since 1980.

Figure 1. Bureaucracy in Netherlands

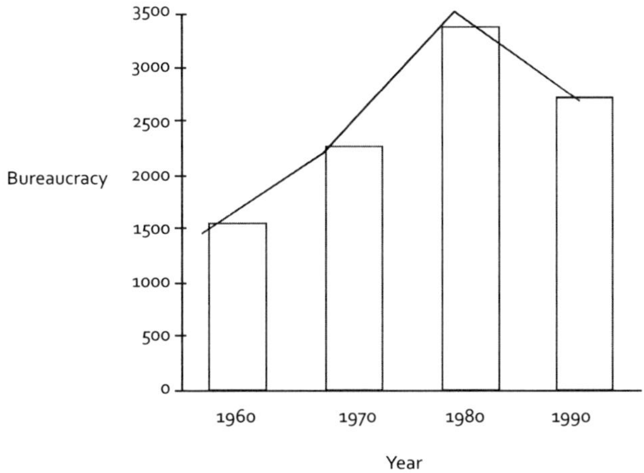

Figure 2. Quagocracy in Netherlands

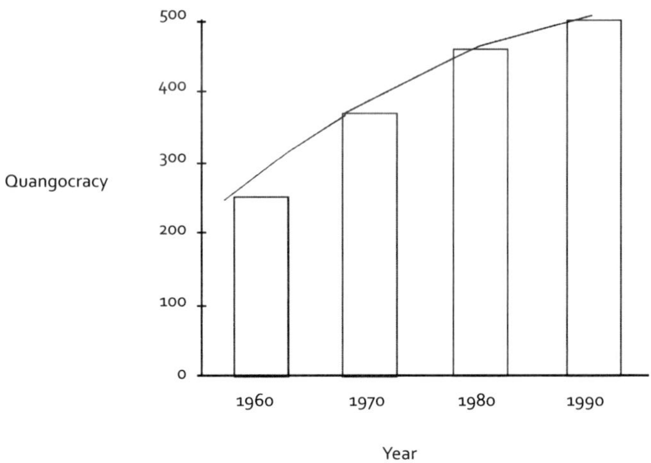

Sources: Adapted from Lee. (2007, 189)

With the pressure to downsize the public government due to the influence of NPM, quagos are increasingly replacing departmental organizations. The Organization for Economic Cooperation and Development (OECD) recently estimated that arm's length bodies in central governments now account for 50 percent of public expenditure and public employment in OECD countries (OECD, 2003, 5).

The critical motives behind the growing number of quagos are:

> 1)The belief (policy theory) that efficiency of government will increase when tasks are carried out by quagos instead of the central government; and
> 2) The belief that quagos will reduce the distance between policies and people/society (Flinders et al., 74).

With NPM, there are several theories which explain the phenomena of the rapid rise of the quagos.

According to New Institutional Economics which serves as the background of NPM, quagos are being chosen because they are more efficient organizations than traditional bureaucracies (Pollitt et al., 2003, 13) Taliercio (2004) offers an example of rational choice analysis which explains the choice of the quago form on the grounds that it leads to greater efficiency (in this case, efficiency in revenue collection in developing countries). Based on these studies, we could surmise that the growth of quagos results from the belief that they are more efficient in terms of public management and they are better at serving people's needs.

Local Quagos' Growth in Korea

Local governments produce and deliver public services to the citizen. Local quagos are responsible for spending large amounts of local governments' budgets and employing a substantial percentage of the local population. In other words, local quagos are good for the local economy if they demonstrate excellence in management.

Unfortunately, information on the number and activities of local quagos has never been collected. Privatization and quagocratization are often considered preferable alternative approaches for the provision of municipal goods and services, but actual figures are not cited. (Leeuw and Theil, 1999, 72).

In Korea, local quagos are composed primarily of local special accounts (Direct Management by local government) and local public corporations; so far, there are no local agencies or privatizing public corporations in Korea. The Korean local quagos are not as diverse as the national ones.

Figure 3 shows us that the number of local quagos has been increasing—from 7 units in 1970 to 367 units in 2007. Especially after 1995, when the reform in favor of local autonomy came into force in Korea, the number of local quagos has expanded rapidly. The functions of establishing local quagos and appointing their CEOs have been delegated from the central government to the local government.

Such decentralization has provided momentum for the creation of local quagos. Political and administrative decentralization has been a cause of the increasing number of local public institutions and local public enterprises (so called Indirect Management). Table 5 shows us that the number of local public institutions and local public enterprises has grown by 985.7 percent and 338.1 percent, respectively, while the number of local special accounts (so called Direct Management) has grown only by 182.6 percent.

The main reason why the number of the local public institutions has increased rapidly is quagocratization—many local departmental organizations, such as garbage disposal and environmental affairs bodies, are being replaced by local public institution style organizations.

The second reason why the number of the local quagos has increased is that local politicians and bureaucrats are eager to extend their political influence through autonomous local government. Decentralization of the competency of creation and the CEO appointing authority of the local quagos stimulated them to establish wholly local government owned public corporations and local public enterprises.

Figure 3 shows that the number of wholly government-owned local public enterprises has been increasing, while the number of mixed public/private-owned local public enterprises with less than 50 percent public ownership has been decreasing. Even though decentralization measures in 'the revised local public enterprise law' were intended originally to increase the number of mixed-style local public enterprises, the result has not met expectations. This suggests that local politicians and bureaucrats prefer entirely government-owned local public enterprises over mixed public/private-owned local public enterprises. The former type is better for funding and public control of the budget, organization and personnel. The local politicians and bureaucrats do not like persuading private businessmen to invest, nor do they want private businessmen to interfere in public enterprises.

The third reason for the local quagos' growth deals with imitation and trend following. When a local self-governing body creates a public corporation, other bodies tend to follow suit. A look at the example presented in Table 5 will help clarify this point. There were only 5 local development corporations at the highest level of local government in 1995, whereas 16 local development corporations exist today (2008) at the higher and lower levels of local government. Regardless of the necessity of setting up public corporations, lower level local governments tend to copy the higher level local governments in creating local development corporations. With the example of the Korean local public enterprises, the creation of local quagos has occurred mainly through imitation rather than through an assessment of need. Mimic institutionalism is thus a powerful explanation.

The fourth reason for local quagos' growth is that it represents a side effect of public employee downsizing. Despite relatively small sizes of local government, the financial crisis of 1997 forced Korean local governments to cut off a certain percentage of staff. The number of local public government employees has decreased by 17.3 percent since the public sector restructuring began under the 1998 International Monetary Fund restructuring agreement with Korea. It is extremely difficult to fire public employees in Korean context where the social protection network is weak.

Figure 3.

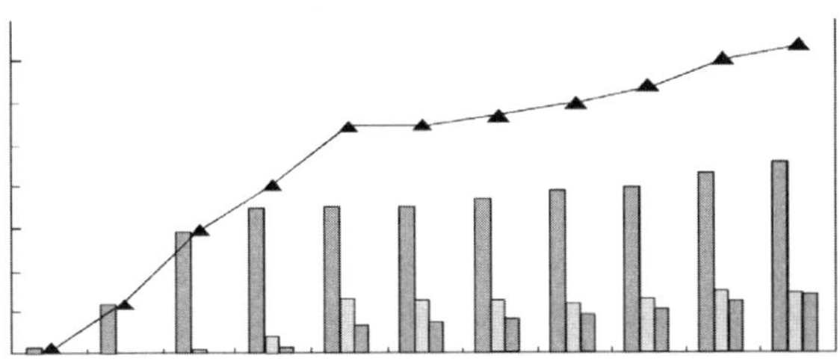

Sources: Ministry of public affairs and safety (1970–2007).

Therefore, many local public employees who were downsized were transferred to local quagos. The decline in the number of local public sector employees has been accompanied by an increase in the number of employees working for local quagos (Yeo and Lee, 2008).

Local Quagos' Efficiency and Accountability

How to Interpret the Phenomena

It is hard to understand social phenomenon in a strictly objective way. Instead everything is more or less subjective. Social Constructivism (a kind of Neo-Institutionalism) denies the traditional classified reality of the organization but emphasizes local culture, regionally prevalent norms and beliefs. Thus traditionally embedded relations between Department-Quagos-Local Government-Local Quagos-Lower level local autonomous bodies play an important role.

Social Constructivism insists Quagos may be part of a wider, but fairly fixed repertoire of administrative proverbs, where choice within the set typically oscillates over time, from one position to another (Hood, 1998).

According to Social Constructivism, various mechanisms of copying and trend following occupy the center attention when attempting to explain the spread of Quagos. It highlights the idea that organizational patterns may spread not because of some inherent efficiency but is a totally different proposition from NPM.

Most OECD countries have created non-commercial bodies outside of the core public sector on an *ad hoc* basis, resulting in an administrative 'zoo'. This has reduced the transparency of government for citizens and compromised oversight and accountability within government (OECD, 2003, 9).

Kicker (2001) analyzes the differences between public and private organizations and concludes that the devolution of authority to semi-autonomous organizations has created a new category of 'hybrid' organization with which neither private sector management principles nor traditional public sector norms work very well.

Our knowledge of quagos lags behind our knowledge of other forms of organizations. Quagos bring positive and negative aspects to the implementation of public policy with some performance exceptionally well while others clearly failing.

The structure of the quago itself does not guarantee net benefits or net costs. Only a detailed look at individual cases can produce such a determination (Michell, 1999).

Traditional governmental organizations have become more efficient in management and more responsive to customers in Korea. Decentralization of the local quagos has been increasing more rapidly than those of national quagos. We expect that such an organizational transformation will invite efficiency through business-like management structures, enhanced accountability, and reduced political intervention.

But questions remain about whether local quagos are in fact more efficient from a managerial (micro)/ socio-economic (macro) perspective and more accountable than democratic control. The local quagos have sometimes been criticized as providing nothing more than well-paid jobs for local residents (Flinders, 1999).

Management Efficiency of the Local Quagos

Efficiency may sometimes be the primary reason for quagos' creation, even though in other instances it is not. Let's examine the efficiency of different types of local quagos in Korea: the local special account (direct management by the local government), the local public institution (indirect management by a special legal entity) and the local public enterprise (also indirect management by a special legal entity).

For the local special account, the water supply and the development fund are keeping the balance in the black by USD 59 million (Ministry of Public Affairs and Safety, 2008). For local public institutions, all local public facilities are in the red by USD 18 million (Ministry of Public Affairs and Safety, 2008). For local public enterprises, the subway and other corporations, except the public development corporations, are in the red by USD 720 million (Ministry of Public Affairs and Safety, 2008).

In Korea, local public institutions and local public enterprises, whose numbers have grown rapidly with decentralization, are in the red while local special accounts are in the black. This means that public institutions, which have evolved from department-style organizations to single-purpose institutions, and local public enterprises, which were created by politicians and civil servants based on their self-interest, are not good structures in terms of management efficiency. Granovetter (1985), in his classic article, refers to this as the problem of the "embeddedness" of economic action.

The use of agencies has become fashionable and has acquired advocates internationally (Pollitt et al., 2003). Interpretative/social constructivists (at least, those of the 'neo-institutionalist' school) have directed attention to the way in which organizational forms spread not because of some inherent efficiency, but through various mechanisms of imitation and trend following (Pollitt, 2002;

Powell and DiMaggio, 1991).

Many local development corporations in Korea seemed to have been established by the mechanisms of imitation and trend following, according to the view of interpretative/ constructivists. We can see that local development corporations are keeping the balance in the black, especially among Korean public enterprises. The lower level local self-governing bodies, which are interested in self-financing, have established and are preparing to create local development corporations even though the higher local autonomy bodies have established them already in the same area.

For example, Gyungsan City, which is a lower level autonomous body, when compared to the higher level autonomous provincial government (Gyeongsangbuk-do), is creating its own development corporation even though Gyeongsangbuk-do has had and operated a development corporation for some time now. Gyungsan City insists that Gyeongsangbuk-do has taken rights and interests in relation to development in its area. Yongin City, Hanam City and Kimpo City in Gyeonggi-do have all established their own development corporations recently. The lower level local self-governing bodies, which have quago-creation authority due to the decentralization measures of the local autonomy system of 1995, copied such previous bodies' examples.

Quago-department relations at the national and local levels may reflect the historically embedded attitudes and norms that characterize a particular ministry; in other words, they are largely path-dependent (Gaints, 2004). Successful public development corporations have come into existence near the capital Seoul and Gyeonggi-do, where land development and housing demand are increasing.

The problem with the proliferation of public development corporations is that redundancy at each autonomous level can divert public resources; Lee et al. (2006) call this issue 'the paradox of the local quago'. The paradox states that if every local self-governing body creates more local quagos, then aggregate social resources will decrease, which will lower total efficiency at the national level.

To reduce the conflict between higher and lower local governments, Ikl (1987) suggests negotiations between the relevant local governments in areas where their interests and rights conflict, a sharing of existing profits, normalization of the abnormal situation, redistribution of profits, innovation and reduction of side effects.

To prevent the paradox of the local quago, it is necessary that the higher and lower levels of local self-governing bodies establish only one public development corporation together at the higher government level through negotiation. The higher government level should allow the lower government level to participate in decision-making related to the management and redistribution of the profits. To do so, they should work together to expand existing profits through normalization of the embedded abnormal situation and to reduce chronic side effects.

Optimal Control of the Local Quagos

Pierr (2004) looks for factors which explain the longevity of the Swedish agency system, and, in particular, identifies a range of influences, both formal and informal, which constrain the apparently large degree of independence which Swedish agencies enjoy. But the independence which quagos enjoy should be accompanied by accountability. Optimal autonomy and optimal control are prerequisites for the accountability of local quagos.

With respect to monitoring quagos, rational choice theory and principal agent theory have a lot to say about how they should be monitored, and this can be translated into a set of principles for designing contracts (Lane, 2000). The agents who are managers as well as employees of quagos should be regularly evaluated on the basis of their performance by the principal who is a citizen or public representative, i.e., local politicians.

Many Korean local quagos have not only been created, but also strongly influenced or directed by local politicians and self-interested officials. This is one method of bureaucratic expansion. It is logical to say that local quagos are owned to some degree by the local government. It has indeed nothing to do with the idea of NPM whose goal is to rescue the public sector by distancing itself from bureaucratic inertia.

But the management of the quagos should be flexible, independent and autonomous from the politicians and bureaucrats. To secure the local quagos' independence but maintain accountability, the current control and oversight system should change to a contract system. The CEO and the staff should carry out their duties under a contract without politicians and higher ranking officials interfering.

As administrative guidance is a powerful tool in Korean society, local officials maintain influence on quagos' activities in various ways. Their influence can be leadership, management, pricing, staffing, financing, etc. Any unnecessary directions or demands, besides those contained in the contract, by higher and lower local governments should be forbidden.

Human resource management is particularly important for quagos' optimal operation. Merit based systems of personnel administration, as opposed to spoils systems, can be considered as the panacea for assuring accountability in quagos. The management performance of local quagos should be linked to an incentives system. Payment and terms for managers, including the CEO, of the local quagos should be based on management performance.

The management of the local quagos should be autonomous, but its accountability should be governed strictly by contract.

Framework of Analysis for Quagos' Position in the More Autonomous Public Sector Map

The information below provides an analytical framework to help understand the various types of quagos. Some degree of disaggregation (structural independence and separation from the ministry or department) and some degree of flexibility/autonomy (discretion/freedom in use of finances, organization or personnel) are both defining criteria for organizations in the More Autonomous Public Sector. This can be related with political ideology. The More Autonomous Public Sector Map could be placed in a continuum from the strictly public organization on the left (which emphasizes the ideology of public interest) to market style organization on the right (which pursues entrepreneurship and autonomy).

Degree of Disaggregation and Characteristics of the National Quagos

The types of national quagos can be mapped out such as ministry/department → special account → agency → public corporation → privatizing corporation.

First of all, it is important to dispose of a special account which separates quagos from the general budget. There are four special accounts in Korea: post business and post bank account (both of which are carried out by an operational division of the

Korea Post), grain management (carried out by a section of the ministry for food, agriculture, fishery and forest), and procurement (carried out by a bureau of the public procurement service). The special accounts are regulated mainly by the national financial law in finance, the government organizational law in organization, and the national government employee law in personnel.

The second type of quago is an agency. This is an organizational entity which operates in its own way. The United Kingdom Next Steps Agencies, Japanese Independent Corporations (IACs), Canadian Special Operating Agencies (SOAs) are some examples of agencies (Pollitt et al., 10).

In Korea, an agency is classified as either an administrative style agency or an entrepreneurial style agency and governed by the government enterprise law, government organizational law, national government employee law and operating law of agencies in finance, organization and personnel. There are 26 administrative style agencies as of 2008, such as the Intellectual Property Office, Local Statistical Office, National Museum of Contemporary Art and National Institute of Scientific Investigation, and 20 entrepreneurial style agencies as of 2008, such as Local National Hospitals and Drivers' License Agencies.

This naturally leads to perhaps the most well known form of quago; public corporations. Between the polar opposites of government bureaucracy and private corporations rests a dizzying array of public corporations. Public corporations are hybrids, having some of the freedom from rules and regulations that the private sector enjoys but retaining some of the accountability and responsiveness of government agencies (Mitchell, 1999).

In Korea, public corporations can be classified as quasi-departmental institutions or public enterprises. The quasi-departmental institution is focused on the value of the public interest rather than entrepreneurship. The public enterprise is more autonomous than the quasi-departmental institution in finances, organization and personnel.

The quasi-departmental institution usually accomplishes a nationally entrusted mission and public fund management instead of the government. The public enterprise administers monopolistic public utilities and similar enterprises.

The public enterprise is further divided into market style corporations and semi-market style corporations. The market style corporation is larger in size and has a better ability to sustain its management team than the semi-market style corporation.

In Korea, there are 305 public corporations as of 2008, which include 77 quasi-departmental institutions, 24 public enterprises and 204 other types.

The last type of quago is a private company. A privatizing corporation is an organization, which has been privatized partially, is in the process of privatization or is ready to be privatized in the near future. This has organizational and personnel systems that operate between those of public enterprises and general business corporations under the company law or commercial corporation law.

In Korea, there are 6 privatizing corporations as of 2008, such as the Korea Gas Corporation and the Korea Airport Corporation.

Characteristics of the quagos at the national level are as follows:

Table 1. Characteristics of National Quagos

Criteria		Ministry/ Department	Special Account	Agency	Public Corporation	Privatizing Corporation
Finance	flexibility and autonomy	Strict (general account)	more flexible than general account	a kind of special account	more flexible than agency	more flexible than public corporation
	resolution	national assembly	national assembly	national assembly	board of directors	board of directors
	relevant law in Korea	national financial law	government enterprise law	government enterprise law/ operating law of agencies	operating law of public corporations	privatization law
Organi-zation	form	government bureau or section	government bureau or section or operational division	operational division	Legal person	legal person
	resolution	national assembly	national assembly	national assembly	board of directors	board of directors
	relevant law in Korea	government organiza-tional law	government organiza-tional law	government organiza-tional law/ operating law of agencies	creation law of the focal corporation/ operating law of public corporations	creation law of the focal corporation/ privatization law/commer-cial law
Person-nel	status	government employee	government employee	government employee, but CEO is a contracting specialist	staff member of the corporation	staff member of the corporation
	resolution	national assembly	national assembly	national assembly	board of directors	board of directors
	relevant law in Korea	national government employee law	national government employee law	national government employee law/ operating law of agencies	creation law of the focal corporation/ operating law of public corporations	creation law of the focal corporation/ privatization law/ commercial law

Table 2. Local Quagos according to Degree of Political Control

Public Interest--Entrepreneurship
Local Ministry/Department
→ Local Special Account
→ Local Agency
→ Local Public Corporation
→ Local Privatizing Corporation

Degree of Disaggregation and Characteristics of the Local Quagos

Some degree of structural disaggregation from the local ministry or department, some degree of flexibility in finances, independence of organization and autonomy of personnel are also defining criteria for local quagos, which are similar to those of national quagos. The types of local quagos can be mapped out along the following political continuum (Table 2).

Local Special Account (Direct Management)

The working definition of a local special account is the same as that of the national government. It is usually called Direct Management, since it is owned and run by the local government directly. It is more flexible than the local general account budget, though it must be approved by the local parliament like general accounts. The CEO and employees who execute it are all public servants.

In Korea, there are 227 local special accounts as of 2008,

which are made up of 108 water services, 64 sewage treatment plants, and 55 development funds.

Local Agency

The working definition of a local agency is the same as that of the national government.

In Korea, there are no local agencies currently, but the Seoul Metropolitan City government plans to change the current directly controlled businesses of Water Services, City Museum, Historical Museum and Transportation BroaD.C.asting to local agencies (JoongAng Ilbo, 2008. 5. 20).

Local Public Corporation (Indirect Management)

The working definition of a local public corporation is the same as that of the national government. But the specific forms are slightly different. Local public corporations are divided into public institutions, which are wholly owned by the local government, and public enterprises, which are constructed as public-private entities with more than half of the capital owned by the local government. These kinds of public corporations are called Indirect Management, since they are owned by the local government but run by separate legal entities indirectly.

The public institution's budget is autonomous, with deliberations and resolution carried out by its board of directors, but the budget sometimes has to be approved by the chief of the local government. The CEO is a specialist recommended by the board of directors (or special recommendation committee) and appointed by the chief of the local government.

The public enterprise's budget is much more autonomous,

with deliberations and resolutions carried out solely by the board of directors. The CEO is a specialist recommended and appointed by the board of directors and sometimes approved by the chief of the local government.

In Korea, there are 140 public corporations as of 2008, which include 69 public institutions (such as the Facilities Management Corporation) and 71 public enterprises (such as Local Transportation Corporations, Local Public Hospitals, and Local Development Corporations) (Ministry of Public Administration and Safety, 2008).

Local Privatizing Corporation

The working definition of a local privatizing corporation is the same as that of the national government, but there is no local privatizing corporation in Korea.

Almost all the characteristics of the local quagos are the same as those of the national quagos. But the local quagos in Korea are regulated by the Local Public Enterprise Law, while the national quagos are controlled by each quago's governing laws. Characteristics of local quagos, except where they are the same as the national quagos, are detailed in Table 3.

Table 3. Characteristics of the Local Quagos

Criteria	Local Ministry/ Depart-ment	Local Special Account (direct management)	Local Public Corporation (indirect management)	
			Local Public Institution	Local Public Enterprise
Con-cept	core orga-nization of local gov-ernment	local public busi-ness owned and run by local government directly	local public institution owned wholly by the local government but run by a separate legal entity	local public enterprise with more than a half of the stock owned by the local government but run by a separate legal entity
Finance	strict (general account) under local parliament' resolution	more flexible than the local general account budget but spending approved by local parliament, like the general account	autonomous budget spending by board or director resolution (sometimes approved by the chief of the local government)	much more autonomous budget spending by board or directors' resolution
	-	local government bond for special account	corporate bond	corporate bond
	-	revert to the local government treasury	revert to the local government treasury	revert to investors
Organi-zation	bureau or section of the local department	bureau or section or operational division of the local department	a kind of legal public organization	a kind of stock company
	local autonomy law	local government	local government	mixed public and private investors
	dependent on the local parliament	nominally independent from local government control	moderately independent from local government control	strongly independent from local government
Person-nel	public servant	public servant	staff member of the institution	staff member of the enterprise
	public official appointed by the chief of the local govern-ment	public official appointed by the chief of the local government	specialist recommended by the board of directors and appointed by the local governor	specialist recommended and appointed by the board of directors (sometimes approved by the local governor)

Conclusion

One reason for the shortcomings of international comparative research on quagos lies in the use of ambiguous terminology and the absence of a coherent classification of the variety of quagos' forms (OECD, 2003).

In spite of such limitations, this chapter examined empirically why the number of local quagos is increasing and explored some negative implications of the growth of local quagos internationally and in Korea.

This chapter discovered that the number of the Korean local quagos expanded after 1995, when the local autonomy system was put into effect and that the number of quagos has increased in Western countries since the 1980s due to the implementation of NPM theory. The main reason for the significant increase in the number of local quagos in Korea is 'quagocratization' by imitation or trend following, as the social constructivists argue. Local politicians and bureaucrats, eager to extend their political influence, have also contributed to the growth of local quagos in Korea. Both of these reasons have their roots in the decentralization of authority, which created local quagos and appointed their leadership posts as a result of implementation of the local autonomy system.

There are a number of problems created by the rapid growth of local quagos, including socio-economic or managerial inefficiency and issues of accountability.

In terms of the socio-economic efficiency, this chapter suggests that the higher and lower levels of local governments should work together to establish only one quago for the same task or mission and should redistribute the profits generated by the quago.

In terms of managerial efficiency and accountability, this

chapter suggests that the management of local quagos should be autonomous, but its accountability should be ensured through contract. The CEO and managers of the quagos should carry out their mission autonomously without politicians or higher ranking officials interfering, but they should also bear responsibility for their performance through pay and term length determined by contract.

References

JoongAng Ilbo. 2008. *Experiment on Autonomous Management-incentive based on Performance* (2008. 5. 20).

Ministry of Public Administration and Safety. (1970–2008). *Local Public Corporation.*

OECD. 2003. *Public Sector Modernization: Changing Organizations* GOV/PUMA (2003), Paris, 28 October.

Flinders, M.V. 1999. 'Setting the Scene: Quagos in Context', In M., Flinders and M., Smith eds. *Quagos, Accountability and Reform.* New York: St. Martin's Press.

Flinders, M. and M., Smith. 1999. *Quagos, Accountability and Reform,* New York: St. Martin's Press.

Gaints, F. 2004. Adapting the Agency Concept: Variations within "Next Steps", In C. Pollit C. and C. Tallbot. eds. *Unbundled Government,* London: Taylor and Francis. 53–74.

Granovetter, M. 1985. 'Economic Action and Social Structure: The Problem of Embeddedness', *American Journal of Sociology* 91(3): 484–510.

Hood, C. 1998. *The Art of the State: Culture, Rethoric and Public Management,* Oxford: Oxford University Press.

Ikl, F.C. 1987. *How Nations Negotiate,* New York: Kraus Reprint. 22–26.

Kickert, K. 2001. Public Management of Hybrid Organizations: Governance of Quasi-autonomous Executive Agencies, *International Public Management Journal* 4(2): 135–50.

Lane, J.E. 2000. *New Public Management,* Aldershot, Ashgate.

Lee, et al. 2006. A Basic Study on the Transformation Path of Public Organization: Analysis on the Paradox of Local Government Shadow Organization, *Korea Public Administration Review* 40(3).

Lee, S.C. 2007. *Understanding of the Korean Enterprises,* Seoul: Daeyoung Publishing Co.

Leeuw, F.L. and S.V., Theil. 1999. Quagocratization in the Netherlands, Flinders et al. eds. 72–83.

Michell, J. 1999. *The American Experiment with Government Corporations,* New York: M.E. Sharpe, Inc.

Pierr, J. 2004. Central Agencies in Sweden: A Report from Utopia, In C. Pollit and C. Talbot. eds. *Unbundled Government,* London: Taylor and Francis, 203–14.

Pollitt, C. 2002. Clarifying Convergence: Striking Similarities and Durable Differences in Public Management Reform, *Public Management Review* 4(1): 471–92.

_______, J., Caufield, A., Smullen and C., Talbot. 2001. Agency Fever? Analysis of an International Fashion, *Journal of Comparative Policy Analysis* 3: 271–90.

_______, C., Talbot, J., Caulfield and A., Smullen. 2004. *Agencies: How Governments do Things through Semi-autonomous Organizations,* New York: Palgrave Macmillan.

Powell, W. and P., DiMaggio. eds. 1991. *The New Institutionalism in Organizational Analysis,* Chicago, III: University of Chicago Press.

Samuelson, P. 1973. *Economics,* 9th ed. New York: McGraw-Hill.

Taliercio, R. 2004. The Design, Performance and Sustainability of Semi Autonomous Revenue Authorities in Africa and Latin America, In Pollitt, C. and Talbot, C. eds. *Unbundled government,* London: Taylor and Francis, 264–82.

Yeo, Y.H. and S.C. Lee. 2008. 'Growth Problems and Institutional Improvement Measures of Local Public Development Corporations, *Korean Public Administration Quarterly* 20(1): 237–60.

Zartman, W. ed. 1983. *The 50% Solution,* New Haven: Yale University Press, 7–9.

Chapter 9 |

Centralized versus Decentralized Governance of Public Service Delivery

SUNG-BAE KIM

Introduction

Reform of public service delivery is an important component of the Korean government's agenda for government innovation. As the government has revealed its intention, heated disputes have occurred over the optimal form of governance for public service delivery. Particularly, the disputes center on the relative efficiency of two types of governance. The first of the two types is centralized governance which is conducted by using local branches of central government and the other is decentralized governance which is based on the delegation of tasks to local governments. The proponents of each form of governance insist on the superiority of the form they prefer without paying due attention to the alternative. The one-sided presentation of their positions seems to be caused by the lack of an adequate framework upon which a comparison of the forms of governance can be made.

This study attempts to develop a theoretical framework and to assess the contentions made in favor of each position. Specifically, based on incomplete contract theory, the theoretical framework extends it further by incorporating some of the unique features of public sector. We then apply the framework to evaluate the validity of existing contentions in a specific case, i.e., the governance of national road service delivery. This case is selected because the governance of national road service delivery is a prime candidate for reform in Korea. In this respect, the results of this study would be valuable to the Korean government, which is considering a reform of national road service delivery.

In addition, this study has theoretical value as well. Particularly, this study contributes to the expansion of the realm in which incomplete contract theory can be applied (Grossman and Hart, 1986; Hart and Moore, 1990; Hart, 1995). While this theory has been developed mainly for the analysis of firms, some studies have already utilized the theory to address issues in the public sector. Thus far, these studies have more or less focused on addressing the issue of privatization. Notable examples are Shleifer and Vishny (1994), Schmidt (1996), Hart et al. (1997), and Hart (2003). This study, by analyzing the issue of public service delivery, may further broaden the realm of application of incomplete contract theory.

This chapter discusses important issues. It examines the mechanisms currently used by central government for public service delivery in local areas by providing detailed information on local branches of the central government, which are under close scrutiny as they are a major target for reform. It also qualifies contentions regarding the relative efficiency of the two forms of governance for public service delivery; those forms being based either on delegation or using local branches of the central government.

Overview of Public Service Delivery System in Korea

Delivery of Public Services

According to a survey conducted by MOGAHA (Ministry of Government Administration and Home Affairs) in 2002, the total number of types of services that government had to deliver in Korea amount to 41,603 as specified by 3,353 laws (PCGID, 2004). Of these services, central government is responsible for 73 percent (30,240) and local government is responsible for the remaining 27 percent. While the responsibility for the delivery of services can be classified as above, most of them are delivered in one of several ways which are namely direct delivery, delivery by central government's local branches, delegation to local government and contracting out to the private sector.

Table 1 shows the relative importance of each of these delivery methods. Of these methods, direct delivery accounts for the largest proportion, 54.4 percent. Delivery by local branches of the central government and affiliated organizations of central government amounts to 12 percent and 28.8 percent respectively. Of the remainder, delegation to local government accounts for 4.2 percent and contracting out to the private sector just 0.6 percent.

If we look at types of service to which each of these methods is applied, direct delivery is normally applied to services which are associated to the well being and safety of the public such as national defense, foreign affairs etc. Services delivered by central government's local branches or affiliated organizations are those which require a high level of specialization where local government would face difficulties in recruiting qualified personnel. Also included are the services delivered over a specific jurisdiction which

Table 1. Delivery of Public Services

Type of Delivery	Number of Public Services (%)	Governance Type
Total	31,551 (100)	
Direct Delivery	17,172 (54.4)	Centralized Governance
Central Government's Local Branch of the Central Government	3,798 (12.0)	Centralized Governance
Central government's Affiliated Organization	9,090 (28.8)	Centralized Governance
Delegation to Local Government	1,311 (4.2)	Decentralized Governance
Contracting out to Private Sector	180 (0.6)	Decentralized Governance

Sources: Presidential Committee for Government Innovation and Decentralization (2003).

does not correspond to existing administrative boundaries. Unlike these services, delivery of routine services is normally delegated to local government. Included are such services as forest management, agricultural seed supply and small business assistance etc. Finally, while it is still in the incipient stage, there are cases where contracting out to the private sector is used for service delivery. These include the cleaning of buildings and waste disposal.

Local Branch of the Central Government

This section details the main characteristics of central government's local branches. They are the administrative offices established in localities to deliver public services for which the central government is responsible. By law, central government is allowed to establish local branches of central government in order to deliver services that local government may not deliver adequately.

In this context, the number and types of branch offices of

the central government in Korea have continued to increase since 1970. From 1985 to 1995 when the expansion of the organization was most conspicuous, the number more than doubled from 3,058 to 7,247. Since then, the number has declined somewhat since decentralization was re-established from 1995 with the election of each local government's head. According to the government's statistics, the total number of central government's local branches amounts to 6,574 branches established by 24 ministries in 2003. Of these local branches of central government, those for police and public prosecutor services account for the largest portion, 53 percent. The local branches of central government which performs postal work and railway administration accounted for the second largest proportion of 38 percent. Local branches of the central government involved in national tax administration account for 0.1 percent. The remaining 9 percent of the local branches of central governments are for general administration. Currently, it is this arrangement of the central government which deals with general administrative affairs that is the major target of reform.

As it is often alleged, the existence of local branches of central government for general administration is deemed to problematic. Of particular importance is the functional overlap in the delivery of general administrative service between the local branches of central government and local government. The overlap appears to be caused simply because it is almost impossible to have a clear demarcation between services which should be delivered by each type of government. Also, there are no appropriate and clear-cut rules or directives clarifying the type of services whose delivery should be delegated to local government.

Contentions

There are delivery mechanisms which use local branches of the central government and are based on the delegation of issues to local government. Scholars in favor of local branches of the central government insist that the offices should continue to exist (Korean Institute of Public Administration, 2002) due to the superiority of the local branches in terms of staff's specialized skills and the strong incentives it provides.

Others insist that given the fact that local autonomy has been established on a large scale, services delivered by the local branches of the central government must be either transferred or delegated to local government (Presidential Committee on Government Innovation and Decentralization, 2004). They claim that local branches of the central governments may not only result in inefficient service delivery, but also suffer from low accountability to citizens.

The claims made by each side seem to have a sound basis and thus appear to be justified. These are the arguments which need to be further scrutinized using an appropriate theoretical framework. First, we need to examine the arguments raised over the quality of service provided.

On the one hand, the quality of services is low, because the local branches of the central governments are uninformed about local conditions as well as the needs of the residents, and as a consequence they cannot produce high quality services from the local resident's point of view. Also, they are free from the control of local politics and thus do not respond adequately to the needs of local residents.

On the contrary, others claim that if the responsibility of service delivery is delegated to local government, the quality of service will degrade more easily because the quality of service required at the national level and the local conditions which are catered to may not be the same. Thus, local government tends to focus more on the latter quality at the expense of the former and thus causes the quality of service to degrade.

Second, the incentive mechanisms are also an issue. This issue is focused on finding out under which governance arrangement agents involved in service delivery make a larger investment to improve their skills and technical knowledge. These investments are instrumental in improving the performance of agents involved in the process of service delivery. Some claim that local branches of the central governments may invest much into human capital which is specific to the tasks they perform thanks to economies of scale. But others insist that local government may invest more in improving their knowledge and skills specific to local conditions, since they are more informed about local situations and under stronger pressure to meet the needs of local residents.

Finally, there is the issue of accountability in the delivery of public services. It is often claimed that under centralized governance, politicians and bureaucrats are more likely to become involved in bribery and patronage. Since local branches of the central government are located in remote areas and their performances are monitored only by the central ministries and free from local political control, the offices are claimed to be more susceptible to scandal. Whereas, local government is considered more accountable since it is subject to not only central government's monitoring systems, but also local political control. But for the same reason, they may be subject to capture by local elites.

Theoretical Framework of Analysis

In order to develop the theoretical framework, we need to

Figure 1. Public Service Delivery System

Provision ---> Production ---> Consumption

identify a few premises. The first premise concerns the simple but powerful idea that public service delivery can be separated into two distinctive elements. As shown in Figure 1, they are the provision side and production side, each of which can be organized in quite different ways.

The provision side, in general, refers to the choices concerning such decisions as the type of services to be provided, the quantity and quality standards of service to be provided, the amount of revenue to be raised and how to raise it etc. Providers are those in charge of works on the provision side. The production side, as distinguished from provision side, refers to the more technical process of transforming input into output to render a service. Those in charge of these works are referred to as producers. The distinction between the provision and production sides lays the conceptual foundation for a new understanding of the organization of public service delivery. ACIR (Advisory Commission on Intergovernmental Relations) argues in a similar vein that "there is a growing consensus that government has a responsibility to provide services and facilitate this through policies it makes, but services and facilities may be produced by both private and public sectors, based on values of cost effectiveness and equity (ACIR, 1987)."

The second premise is concerned with the idea that the relationship between provider and producer may be represented as an incomplete contract relationship. The incompleteness of the relationship is not hard to see once it is recognized that the quality of service the government wants often cannot be fully specified. In fact, it is difficult to identify and specify the quality characteristics of a public service prior to service delivery. This is because some of the information relevant to the delivery may be unobservable by one or more of the parties. Also, it may result from the fact that some information, although observable by the parties, may not be specifiable as part of the conditions of the relationship.

While it may be possible for analytic purposes to distinguish the provision and production sides, we need to combine them in some way to actually deliver public services. For example, we may integrate them so that the same organization assumes roles as both provider and producer. In other cases, we separate them so that different organizations assume the role as provider and producer respectively. What is important is that the efficacy of public service delivery can be significantly affected by the way the two sides are organized. The following discussion is concerned with the development of theoretical framework upon which we assess the relative efficacy of organizational arrangements.

Case of the National Road Services

In this case study, I apply the aforementioned theoretical framework to evaluate the relative efficacy of governance arrangements for national road service delivery. Particularly, I will compare the traditional delivery system using the local branches of the central governments with the newly proposed one which is based on delegation of responsibilities to local governments. It is with this comparison that I will be able to evaluate the validity of the contentions raised against each of these delivery systems.

Korean Context

Some information on the specificity of the Korean context should be provided in order to facilitate the following discussions. To begin with, it is noted that the delivery of national road services is made in two distinctive ways. First, while the provision decision is made by the Ministry of Construction and Transportation (MOCT), the services are actually produced by the local branches of the central government of the ministry. The other delivery arrangement is to delegate service production to local governments, while the responsibility of service provision remains in the hands of the MOCT. The former is considered centralized governance and the latter as decentralized governance. Under the former arrangement, the residual control rights are given to central government, while in the latter case control rights are given to local governments. As for the role of each party, the provider is responsible for establishing national road policy, planning for road management and construction, and the allocation of road resources. The role of the producer includes operation of machinery, equipment and various facilities, management of road maintenance and repairs, permission to use road sideways, and designation and change of road areas.

The organizational characteristics of producers in each system can also be distinguished. Under the centralized arrangement, 24 local branches of the central government, located across the nation, are responsible for the production of national road services. This implies that each organization has to manage approximately 650km of national roads. Under the decentralized arrangement, production responsibility is delegated to either provincial governments or municipal governments. If delegated to provincial governments, 9 provincial governments produce national road maintenance services. If delegated to municipal governments, 230 governments produce the service. Thus, each government is responsible for the management of 1,730km and 68km of national roads respectively.

Finally, we need to pay attention to the structure of agency relationships among the participants involved in the delivery of national road service. Figure 1 shows the relationship under centralized governance. Seen from the principal agent's perspective, the MOCT as an agent is under a principal agent relationship with politicians. The MOCT is also under a principal agent relationship with local branches of the central government, in principal. While the extent of the relationship may vary, most agents are under a principal agent relationship with local residents. The agency relationship under decentralized governance becomes more complicated than those under centralized governance. Figure 2 shows the agency relationship under decentralized governance. As under centralized governance, the MOCT has a principal agent relationship with the national legislative body.

The local government as service producer is under multiple principal agent relationships with the MOCT, local legislative body, and local residents. Finally, local residents as the principal are under a principal agent relationship with the national legislative body, the MOCT, local government, and local legislative body.

Figure 2. Agency Relationship under Centralized Governance

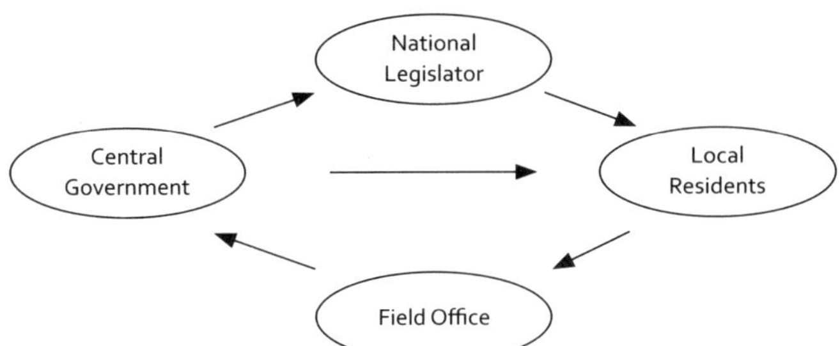

Figure 3. Agency Relationship under Decentralized Governance

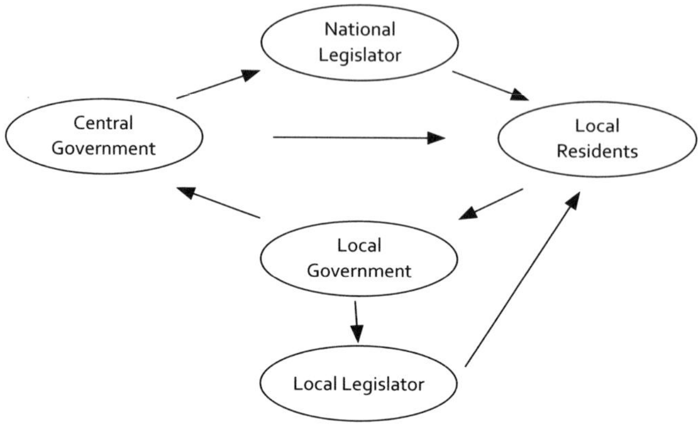

Discussion

The relative efficacy of the two governance arrangements can be evaluated with respect to many aspects. As mentioned previously, however, we may select a few issues of major importance arising from the existence of the dual delivery arrangements. Particularly, this study focuses on the issues concerning the quality of services and the incentive structure for agents involved in the delivery of national road service. We also consider the issue of corruption which is often cited as a major problem.

_Quality of Services

The first issue to be addressed is the quality of national road service. We select this issue because of the contention that under decentralized governance the quality of service can easily be degraded. The basis for this contention is that due to the nature of local politics, the decisions made by the head of a local government may often be detrimental to the quality of national road service.

For example, we often find too much development permitted by this public figure in the areas around national roads which results in the functional deficiency of the roads as major artery. Moreover, since the roads are managed separately by many local governments, the quality of service may be low if coordination among the governments is not secured properly.

Before we evaluate this contention, we need to define the attributes comprising road service quality. Although the quality of road service comprises of many attributes, we focus on the two major attributes of accessibility and mobility. Mobility here implies the ability of individuals using the road to move between different regions, while accessibility refers to how easy it is to reach national roads. It is often the case that mobility and accessibility face constant trade-offs in their relationship. For example, improving accessibility may require many connecting roads, but mobility deteriorates with the number of connecting roads. The trade-off between mobility and accessibility becomes the heart of the controversy over the quality of national road service.

As contended, it seems true that decentralized governance may deliver a lower quality national road service than centralized governance. This is because the national road service is considered as an important physical asset, and non-human assets a_1 and a_2 are normally complementary, therefore it is under centralized governance that the levels of effort made by both provider and producer should be higher, and thus the overall quality of road service can be higher. The provider as the possessor of the residual control rights tends to make more of an effort and perform better under centralized governance. The producer, as a subsidiary of the provider, can also have an incentive structure similar to the provider. It is also under centralized governance that both provider and producer can make more relationship specific investments and raise the level of human capital to a higher level.

The superiority of centralized governance can also be determined by the agency relationship in national road service delivery. As previously shown, we may recall that the participants in the delivery of national road service lie in a multiple principal agent relationship. In the situation where there are many principals, the incentive of the participants becomes weaker than otherwise. The problem of weak incentive can be particularly serious under decentralized governance, where there are many principals which include the central government, local residents and local legislative bodies, etc. as shown in Figure 2. These principals may often deliver conflicting signals. For example, while it is likely that central government will focus on securing maximum mobility, local residents may demand better accessibility. The upshot could be weak incentives for all participants in the delivery of national road service.

Low quality of service may also result from the multiple attributes of road service delivery especially under decentralized governance. Recall the theoretical discussion on the incentive structure for agents who perform multiple tasks. If the quality of one attribute is poorly observable, the incentive for the competing attributes must be weak. Otherwise, there may be an excessive diversion of efforts away from servicing the latter attribute to a more observable one. This argument can be applied precisely to the case of national road service delivery. As discussed previously, the attributes of national road services comprise of mobility and accessibility. Since the benefit of mobility may accrue in much broader areas, the quality of mobility may not be easily observable. The benefit of improved accessibility, however, may be easily felt by the residents at the point of access. In addition, local residents may strongly desire better accessibility instead of mobility. In fact, mobility may often harm the local economy, because some economic activities may relocate to other areas due to improved mobility. Thus, local governments as the producers may focus on improving accessibility, and thereby lowering the overall quality of national road service delivered.

One final caution is in order. The argument above needs to be qualified, depending upon whether the production responsibility is delegated to provincial government or municipal government. If the authority is given to municipal government, there will be some diversion of efforts towards improving accessibility at the cost of mobility and thereby reducing the overall quality of national road service delivered. If the authority is given to provincial governments, such diversion may not be a serious problem. This is because the demand for better accessibility at a particular access point cannot be critical factor in provincial level politics. Therefore, the overall quality of national road service may be sustained.

Relationship Specific Investment

The second issue to be addressed is the level of relationship specific investment made by provider and producer. This investment refers to that which creates value if the agents' relationship extends over time, but does not if the agents split up (Hart, 1995). This investment may involve two dimensions in the context of national road service delivery. One is the investment made at the organizational level. The provider's investment may include establishing a plan for replacing old road sign systems or improving road pavement, etc. The producer's investments may comprise of establishing a strip in the middle of roads or guardrails at the fringe of roads. Another is the investment made by the individuals working in provision and production units. Investment to acquire special skills or knowledge to deliver better road service can be good examples.

As for the relationship specific investment, it is certain that the level should be higher under centralized governance. Under this governance arrangement, both provider and producer have strong incentives to make relationship-specific investments. The provider, as the possessor of residual control rights, can have higher marginal return and thus he invests more. This is because, as discussed previously, not only does the delivery of national road service require a high level of physical assets, but also non-human assets of the provider and producers are complementary because of the technical nature of national road service delivery.

The producer's incentive should also be high under centralized governance, although it is normally claimed that the producer, without residual control rights, may have weak incentives for making relationship-specific investments. This is because unlike the case of private firms, the local branches of the central government are subsidiaries of the MOCT, and thus the members of the offices have an incentive structure similar to those of the MOCT. They may be mindful of their long term career as well as possibilities for promotion and level of payment. There is no reason to believe that the producer's incentive to make relationship-specific investments will be weak under centralized governance.

However, the structure of incentives under decentralized governance reveals quite the opposite. To begin with, the incentive to make relationship specific investments by the MOCT can be weaker than incentives under centralized governance. This is because the MOCT, without residual control rights, may have a much smaller return from their investment than before. Under decentralized governance, the MOCT has to overcome larger transaction costs in the delivery of national road service because the residual control rights are given to local government. Local governments as service producers may also have a weak incentives to make relationship specific investments due to the fact that local government is also responsible for the maintenance of local roads. Thus its investments have to be distributed over national roads as well as local roads. This implies that its investment should be solely focused on delivery of national road services. For example, the technology and material used for the maintenance of national roads may be different from those of local roads, since national roads are normally burdened by a heavy volume of traffic and high speed limits.

In addition, the incentive structure for the individual workers in production units is also weak under decentralized governance. Since local government as a producer normally performs general administrative work, the individual workers in the organization do not have a strong incentive to invest in the improvement of the skills specifically needed for the delivery of national road service because they may have to change their position after a specified period. In fact, this is the major point set forth by those who insist on the superiority of centralized governance for national road service delivery.

_Corruption

The final issue to be addressed concerns the behavior of politicians and bureaucrats. Here we relax the assumption that the bureaucrats and politicians act on behalf of society and allow for them to be self-interested. Given this behavioral assumption, it is not difficult to see that corruption by politicians and bureaucrats can occur frequently. They may use their control rights either to extract money or campaign contributions for themselves from contractors or to pursue objectives which run counter to the public interest, such as catering to interest groups to gain support in elections.

In Korea, it is well known that the most serious source of corruption for politicians and bureaucrats can be found in construction related affairs, consequently construction and maintenance of national and local roads are the areas most stricken with serious corruption scandals. Not only have national legislators, local legislators and the MOCT as a provider been accused of scandalous activities, but local branches of the central government and local governments as producers have also been implicated in many scandals. Particularly, the local branches of the central government tend to be implicated in corruption because of their special characteristics. They are located in remote areas and monitoring by the MOCT is the only control mechanism. They are also free from local political control, because of their status as central government agencies. For these reasons, these offices are frequently implicated in many scandals related to contracting and subcontracting of construction and maintenance work.

Local politicians and government officials are not free from corruption either. Because of the lack of an effective mechanism of oversight, corruption of local government in the delivery of public services is a serious problem. According to the data published recently by a Korean NGO, construction related corruption has mostly been committed by local politicians and bureaucrats. Of the 180 cases of construction related corruption exposed, 76 cases (42%) were committed by local politicians and bureaucrats (Citizen's Coalition of Economic Justice, 2006).

Given such magnitude of corruption, it is important to examine whether we can find any discernable relationship between the level of corruption and governance arrangement. In fact, there are contentions that under centralized governance politicians and bureaucrats may be more easily involved in corruption. It is also argued that devolution of power to elected local government officials, better informed about local conditions, may reduce corruption, thereby improving public service delivery.

In order to evaluate these arguments, I will first focus on the corruption which takes place under centralized governance. From the theoretical discussion above, we are certain that politicians and bureaucrats may be more prone to corruption under centralized governance, since the return from such behavior to the politician is greater. The typical behavior of politicians may be to use his power to extract money or campaign contributions in return for preferential treatment towards a specific construction company. Larger returns can result because private construction companies, by making the contract with providers, will be in a better position to make a contract with producers as well, if the assets a_1 and a_2 are complementary. This means that the size of the bribe the construction company offers will be larger under centralized governance. Whereas under decentralized governance the incentive to become involved in corruption of politicians and bureaucrats would be weaker, because the return from corruption could be much smaller. This is because most contracts for maintenance work are made separately by each local government under decentralized governance.

Finally, it is noted that if corruption is a serious issue, then we may reduce the severity of corruption by adopting a decentralized method of governance for national road service delivery. In fact, decentralized governance of service delivery may lower the incentive for construction companies to solicit bribes and thus reduce the incentives of politicians and bureaucrats to accept bribes as well. The strong resistance to the introduction of decentralized governance by such interest groups as large construction companies and associations of engineers may be considered an indirect indication of such a possibility.

Policy Implications

Thus far, we have examined the relative efficacy of two governance arrangements for the delivery of public service. We developed a theoretical framework based on incomplete contract theory and applied the framework to the case study of the national road service delivery. In so doing, we also examined the validity of the contentions raised against the two governance arrangements.

We can summarize the major findings from the case study as follows. To begin with, centralized governance appears to be more efficient than decentralized governance in terms of the quality of service provided with some qualifications. Even under decentralized governance, the quality of service may be guaranteed if the provincial government rather than municipal government assumes the role of producer. In addition, it is under centralized governance that the provider tends to make more relationship specific investments, while the incentive of the producer to make investments may not be reduced much. Finally, it must be noted that it is under centralized governance that problems of corruption related to politicians and bureaucrats come to be more serious, because both can potentially receive large amounts of returns.

If we apply these findings when evaluating the validity of the existing contentions, some interesting observations can be made. Contrary to the claims made against decentralized governance, it seems that this form of governance can be a good alternative if we delegate the producer's role to the appropriate level of governmental units. In fact, if we delegate roles to the level of provincial government, we may overcome the limitations posed by both centralized methods of governance as well as decentralized methods governance where roles are delegated to municipal governments, as discussed previously. Moreover, both problems of corruption and the degradation of the quality of service can also be partly resolved under this type of decentralized governance. But this governance arrangement may not be as efficient as the centralized governance in terms of providing incentives to make relationship specific investments.

One final comment is that while the analysis has provided some new insights regarding the relative efficacy between centralized governance and decentralized governance of national road service delivery, the insights should not be the sole criteria on which the policy choice should be made. This is because the efficacy of each governance arrangement may also be affected by other factors to which the study has not paid proper attention. It is with a more detailed study of these factors, that we can make a definite policy choice. We defer such analysis to a future study.

References

ACIR (Advisory Commission on Intergovernmental Relations). 1987. *The Organization of Local Public Economics,* Washington D.C.: ACIR.

Citizens Coalition for Economic Justice. 2006. Special Report on Government Corruption, Seoul: Citizens Coalition for Economic Justice.

Korean Institute of Public Administration. 2002. Plan for the Functional Redistribution between Provincial Government and Central Government's Local Branch, Seoul: Korean Institute of Public Administration.

Presidential Committee on Government Innovation and Decentralization. 2004. Special Report on the Reform of Public Service Delivery, Seoul: Presidential Committee on Government Innovation and Decentralization.

Bardhan, P. and D., Mookherjee. 2000. Capture and Governance at Local and National Levels, *The American Economic Review,* Papers and Proceedings 90(2): 135–39.

Belsey, T. and M., Ghatak. 2003. Incentives, Choice and Accountability in the Provision of Public Services, *Oxford Review of Economic Policy* 19(2): 235–49.

Belsey, T. and S., Coate. 2003. Centralized Versus Decentralized Provision of Local Public Goods: A Political Economy Analysis, *Journal of Public Economics* 87(12): 2611–37.

Bernheim, B.D. and W., Michael. 1986. Common Agency, *Econometrica* 54(4): 911–30.

Burgess, S. and R., Marisa. 2003. The Role of Incentives in the Public Sector: Issues and Evidence, *Oxford Review of Economic Policy* 19(2): 285–300.

Cremer, J., A., Estache and P., Seabright. 1995. The Decentralization of Public Services: Lessons from the Theory of the Firm, In A. Estache. ed. *Decentralizing Infrastructure: Advantage and Limitations,* World Bank Discussion Paper 290, Washington D.C.: World Bank.

Dixit, A.K. 1996. *The Making of Economic Policy: A Transaction-cost Politics Perspective,* Boston, MA: MIT Press.

Dixit, A. 2002. Incentives and Organizations in the Public Sector: An Interpretive Review, *Journal of Human Resources* 37(4): 696–727.

_______. and L., John. 1995. Redistributive Politics and Economic Efficiency, *American Political Science Review* 89(4): 856–66.

Domberger, S. and J., Paul. 1997. Contracting out by the Public Sector: Theory, Evidence, Prospects, *Oxford Review of Economic Policy* 13(4): 67–78.

Grossman, S. and H., Oliver. 1986. The Costs and Benefits of Ownership: A Theory of Vertical and Lateral Integration, *Journal of Political Economy* 94(4): 691–719.

Grout, P.A. and S., Margaret. 2003. The Assessment: Financing and Managing Public Services, *Oxford Review of Economic Policy* 19(2): 215–34.

Hart, O. 1995. *Firms, Contract and Financial Structure,* Oxford: Clarendon Press.

_______. 2003. Incomplete Contracts and Public Ownership: Remarks, and an Application to Public-Private Partnerships, *The Economic Journal* 113(March): C69–C76.

Hart, O. and J., Moore. 1990. Property Rights and the Nature of the Firm, *Journal of Political Economy* 98(6): 1119–58.

Hart, O., A., Shleifer, and R.W., Vishy. 1997. The Proper Scope of Government: Theory and an Application to Prison, *Quarterly Journal of Economics* 112(4): 1126–61.

Holstrom, B. and M., Paul. 1988. Common Agency and Exclusive Dealing, Working Paper, Yale University, School of Management.

_______. 1991. Multi-Task Principal-Agent Analyses: Incentive Contracts, Asset Ownership and Job Design, *Journal of Law, Economics and Organization* 7, Special Issue 24–51.

Jack, W. 2004. The Organization of Public Service Provision, *Journal of Public Economic Theory* 6(3): 409–25.

Jin, J. 1999. Types of Functional Overlap and Criteria for Functional Redistribution: Between Local Branch of the Central Government and Local Government, *Journal of Local Government Studies* 11(2):

103–24.

Kim, I. 2002. The Meaning and Functions of Special Local Administrative Agency, *Local Administration* 51(589): 16–23.

Kim, S. 2006. Methodological Extension of Public Policy Research through Comparative Institutional Analysis, *Korean Policy Studies Review* 15(3): 101–29.

_______. 2006. Optimal Governance Model of Public Service Delivery: With Reference to the Function Redistribution of Central Government's Local Branch, *Journal of Local Government Studies* 18(2): 27–48.

Kolderie, T. 1986. The Two Concepts of Privatization in Service Delivery, *Public Administration Review* 40: 240–46.

Milgrom, P. and J., Roberts. 1992. *Economics, Organization and Management*, Englewood Cliffs, NJ: Prentice Hall.

North, D. 1990. A Transaction Cost Theory of Politics, *Journal of Theoretical Politics* 2: 355–67.

Oakerson, R.J. 1999. *Governing Local Public Economics: Creating the Civic Metropolis*, Oakland, CA: Institute for Contemporary Studies.

_______. 2005. Reform Plan for the Local branch of the central government of Ministry of Construction and Transportation, Seoul: Presidential Committee on Government Innovation and Decentralization.

Robinson, R. and S., David. 2001. Decentralization of Road Administration: Case Studies in Africa and Asia, *Public Administration and Development* 21: 53–64.

Seabright, P. 1996. Accountability and Decentralization in Government: An Incomplete Contract Model, *European Economic Review* 40: 61–89.

Schmidt, K.M. 1996. The Costs and Benefits of Privatization: An Incomplete Contracts Approach, *Journal of Law, Economics and Organization* 12(1): 1–24.

Shleifer, A. and R.W., Vishny. 1994. Politicians and Firms, *Quarterly Journal of Economics* 109: 995–1025.

Walsh, K. 1995. *Public Service and Market Mechanisms: Competition, Contracting and the new Public Management*, New York: St. Martin's Press.

Williamson, O.E. 1985. *The Economic Institutions of Capitalism: Firms, Markets, Relational Contracting*, New York: The Free Press.

_______. 1996. *The Mechanisms of Governance*, New York: Oxford University Press.

_______. 1999. Public and Private Bureaucracies: A Transaction Cost Economic Perspective, *Journal of Law, Economics and Organization* 15(1): 306–42.

Wilson, J.Q. 1989. *Bureaucracy: What Government Agencies do and Why They Do It*, New York: Basic Books.

Chapter 10 |

A New Way of e-Government: Geographic Information and Technology Administration

KWANG JU KIM

Introduction

Local governments in Korea, as well as in other countries which possess similar characteristics, need to develop geographic e-government as a potential government model in this age of cyber governance. In an effort to do so successfully it is necessary to review past experiences in order to discover preferable methods of implementation for GIS in Korean local governments. This study utilizes a situational analysis in order to facilitate understanding the present state of the organizations which are contemplating GIS implementation (Huxhold and Levinsohn, 1995: 57–58).

Recently, internet GIS technology has revealed a new path to geographic e-government (Harder, 1998) as GIS becomes a basis for e-government. For example, Greene (2001) shows how GIS in e-government is applicable to various areas such as economic development, planning and zoning, environmental monitoring, law enforcement, property assessment as well as others areas. GIS is not an isolated island. Instead, to be effective, GIS should be connected to regional information systems (RIS) and public management information systems (PMIS). By connecting GIS to RIS and PMIS, a comprehensive GIS can be developed. With the help of Internet, this comprehensive GIS could have diverse impacts on organization behavior and quality of public services

Using GIS is a computer skill that is on the fast track to becoming a generic application for public administration professionals due to the fact that it is quickly becoming an indispensable attribute. Consequently any job applicant would be wise to acquire such skills (Garson, 2003: 8). The generic computer skills currently pertain to word processing, making spreadsheets, creating graphics or data presentations, database management, e-mail and internet. In addition to these skills, GIS techniques are now also beginning to fall into the category of generic applications.

However, computers are seen as neutral instruments and the role of computer technology in the transformation of public administration is thus neglected (Snellen and van de Donk, 1998). GIS is more than a software package and should instead be considered a problem-solving tool. In isolation, GIS technology is a value-free commodity. Yet it is the principal tool which enables public administrators to determine their decisions (Greisler and Stupak, 2007). In tandem with this argument, Masser (1998: 9–29) regards geographic information as a resource, a commodity, an asset, and a type of infrastructure.

Many researchers (Onsrud and Pinto, 1991; Obermeyer and Pinto, 1994; Huxhold and Levinsohn, 1995; Masser, 1998; O'Looney, 2000) have defined GIS as a computerized information system for collecting, storing, manipulating, analyzing, presenting thematic maps and making decisions that is spatially referenced. GIS could be applied to the public sector for uses such as emergency services and dispatch, land use planning, health-care planning, infrastructure planning, political campaigns, and reapportionment (Carr, 2003: 256–258). Both public- and private-sector applications of GIS continue to expand in response to advances in computer technology.

In Korea, local governments began to construct GISs to improve government productivity and performance. Ironically, the construction of GIS and the revival of local autonomy occurred simultaneously in Korea. With the elections of local congress in 1991 and the election of local government executives in 1995, local autonomy has been revitalized following 30 years' guidance by the central government. Stemming from the revival of local autonomy, various GISs have been constructed at the local level. One major impetus for their construction is that if successfully implemented in an organization, GIS can make the organization more accurate in performing its work. Just like other information technologies, it can serve as a tool for reinventing government in the information age (Heeks, 1999).

A situational analysis such as this could provide contextual information for the successful implementation of GISs. In the following situational analysis, this study will examine the developmental process of GIS, the characteristics of GIS and limitations of GIS applications with regards to Korean local governments. Finally, the study recommends alternative approaches to future GIS for Korean local governments.

A Literature Review

Various GIS issues for public managers have been discussed in relation to GIS and democracy, needs assessment, project planning, access to "public records," liability issues, public and private partnerships, dissemination issues, privacy issues, system requirements and design, organizational issues, institutional issues, political support, GIS pitfalls and other issues (Carr, 2003: 259–267). This study especially focuses on the diffusion of geographic information innovations in local governments in terms of content and process models (Onsrud and Pinto, 1991). The former focuses on specific factors and the latter on the key steps or decisions that are involved in understanding how innovations are diffused.

On a Content Model

A content model focuses on determining those specific environmental, organizational, and interpersonal factors that can facilitate or inhibit the implementation process (Leonard-Barton, 1987). Obermeyer and Pinto (1994: 28–29) summarize eight general content factors: clearly defined goals, sufficient resource allocation top-management support, implementation schedules, competent technical support, adequate communication, feedback capabilities, and responsiveness to clients.

Many researchers (Campbell, 1994; Masser and Campbell, 1993; Ventura, 1995; Budic and Godschalk, 1996; Brown and Brudney, 1998; Kim, 1998) studied the effectiveness of GIS practiced by local governments. Huxhold and Levinsohn (1995) introduced three case studies such as the Urban Information Systems Inter-Agency Committee (USAC) experience (Kraemer and King,

1979), Pinto and Onsrud study (1991) and the Campbell study (1992) which support the premise that "successful GIS implementation depends on much or more successfully dealing with planning, design, and institutional issues as it does on GIS technology"(25).

Based on the case study of 12 local governments in the United Kingdom, Campbell (1994) and Masser and Campbell (1993) found that GIS has had a limited impact upon local governments, even after at least two years' experience and four factors of simple applications, user directed implementation, an awareness of the limitations of the organization and a high degree of stability appeared to enhance the chances of success.

Ventura (1995) studied impediments to effective use of GIS in local governments from technical, organizational, and institutional perspectives. To overcome these impediments, he argues that GISs need to be customized to meet the needs of organizations and conversely organizations will have to adapt to the new generation and usage information. Furthermore, Budic and Godschalk (1996) examined the impact of human factors related to the adoption of GIS in local governments and concluded that perceived relative advantage, previous computer experience, exposure to the technology, and networking are the most significant determinants of employee willingness to use new GIS technology.

On the other hand, Brown and Brudney (1998) evaluate the influence of contracting on the successful implementation and utilization of GIS in a local setting and conclude that, while contracting may offer some advantages, over-reliance on contracting compromises the implementation and outcomes of GIS.

In Korea, Kim (1998) surveyed GIS implementation factors at the level of local government. He found that GIS adoption in local government has been technically oriented with a very low degree of concern given to organizational and human factors and consequently proposes to combine organizational and human factors with technical factors from the beginning stages of GIS in order for it to be successfully implemented in Korean local governments.

On a Process Model

A process model analyzes the key steps or decisions related to understanding how innovations are diffused. Nolan's (1979) stage model of computing growth explains the growth of computing in an organization as an evolution of six stages: Initiation, Contagion, Control, Integration, Data administration, and Maturity. Unlike the Nolan theory of evolutionary stages, the Urban Information Systems (URBIS) project study conducted by the Public Policy Research Organization at the University of California, Irvine, Kraemer et al. (1989) found the decisions of managers had by far

Table 1. A Continuum of GIS Organizations

Simple/Convergent Thinking/Uses ... Complex/Divergent Thinking/Uses
Less Potential for Creativity... ... ... More Potential for Creativity

Single
Department — Shared GIS
Dominated by
Single Department — Multi-Departmental
GIS — Multiagency
GIS — Public-Private
Multiagency GIS

Historical Trend
Early GIS Organization ... Current GIS Organization ... Future GIS Organization?

Sources: Adapted from John O'Looney, *Beyond Maps: GIS and Decision Making in Local Government*, p. 29.

the most significant influence on computing development and use. Furthermore they classified clear patterns of management into 4 different states: skill state, the service state, the strategic state and the mix state.

O'Looney (2000: 29) presents a continuum of GIS organizations within and beyond local government as Table 1.

A Situational Analysis of GIS in Korean Local Governments

The Developmental Process of GIS in Korea

The construction of GIS in Korean local governments began in metropolitan cities such as Seoul, Busan, Daegu and other major cities. From the year of 1988, the city of Daegu invested 4.7 billion won to digitize road maps for GIS. This can be viewed as the beginning of constructing GIS by Korean local governments. In 1993 and 1994, the city of Seoul studied the construction of GIS and issued two report papers on the basic plan of GIS in Seoul. The city of Busan developed a long-term plan for GIS in 1997. Now, all of 16 metropolitan governments are directly or indirectly involved in the construction and utilization of GIS at the metropolitan level.

On the other hand, the central government also organized a national commission for GIS (NGIS). It is composed of 11 ministries of central government (construction and transportation, finance and economy, internal affairs, agriculture and fishery, foreign trade and industry, telecommunication, environment, general administration affairs, science and technology, statistics, forestry). The commission developed the first master plan for the construction of National GIS in 1995 and established the GIS Act of 2000. This master plan has served as the base from which local governments participate in the construction of GIS at the local level.

At the first NGIS stage, central government had guided local governments through the process of introducing GIS by digitizing maps. The second NGIS master plan (2001–2005) focused on the application and utilization of GIS (Ministry of Construction and Transportation, 2000). While local governments are developing their own GIS programs, GIS applications of Korean local governments still remain at an early stage. Kim (1998) surveyed 230 local governments to find out if they constructed GISs. This survey showed that among 185 respondents, 14 local governments (7.6%) had established their own GIS, 28 local governments (15.1%) were considering it, and the rest of the 143 local governments (77.3%) responded that they do not have any plan to construct GIS. This survey result implied that the level of GIS adoption by Korean local governments is not very high. Now, at the beginning of 21st century, all of 16 metropolitan and provincial governments have developed GISs while the GISs of local governments are still in the process of being constructed.

Financial Resources

Most local governments began to construct digital maps for GIS with 50 percent financial assistance from the central government. The role of the central government was crucial. If there were not the financial assistance, local governments may be still considering the construction of GIS. With the help of central government's financial assistance, local governments could construct their digital maps. As such, central government had guided the construction of GIS in local governments.

In Korea, central government has a very strong command on policy making and implementation of GIS in local governments because financial independence rates of local governments are very low. According to the Korea Institute of Public Administration's statistics of 2000, financial independence rates are 88.8 percent for Seoul, 68.3 percent for metropolitans, 44.1 percent for provincial governments and the average is 56.2 percent. In the process of constructing or developing GIS, the central government requests 50 percent matching funds from local governments. In order to obtain the central government's financial assistance, local governments could not help putting themselves under the control of central government. This dependency may prevent local governments from voluntarily scrutinizing various applications of GIS at the local level.

Other GIS Components

One of the major problems of GIS implementation in Korean local governments is weak connections between related components of GIS. For example, weak relationships have existed between planning and implementation, construction and utilization, database construction and maintenance, internal and external demand, central and local governments, technical and managerial aspects, and other areas as well. For its success, GIS requires strong linkages between these related areas. In the same vein, local governments need more GIS professionals to make GIS plans and implement them more efficiently. Kim's (1998) survey shows that only 14 (6.1%) of the 230 local governments have GIS professionals.

In sum, the GISs of Korean local governments belong to the initiation stage or skill state. In this stage, the role of information technology is peripheral, the role of information systems is weak and its utility remains at a low level for the time being. These characteristics of GIS limit the application of GIS to Korean local governments. For example, some local governments in Korea such as Kwacheon City, Changwon City, Chungju City and other cities had already constructed their GISs as separate model cases. After that, they expanded their GIS to urban information systems (UIS), which is a conglomeration of all the separate GIS projects. As O'Looney's continuum shows, single departments have adopted GIS in Korea. As a separate program, GIS in local governments could be judged a success. However, more consideration should be given to the evaluation of GIS applications at the level of local government. Before expanding GIS into UIS, we need to examine its implementation by local governments.

Weaknesses of GIS Applications to Korean Local Government

In this section, this study explores the weaknesses that Korean local governments should overcome in order to successfully exploit GIS. Limitations such as technical limitations, organization behavioral and cultural limitations, legal and institutional limitations and database related limitations are of particular interest. Any mishandling of these limitations could lead to the failure of GIS in local governments.

Technical Limitations

The first limitation arises from the low understanding of GIS technology. Local governments need to prepare sufficiently technical aspects before they begin to construct their GIS. The most common mistake is that Korean local governments' officials began to study GIS techniques during the construction period of GIS, however while they construct their GISs, they often realize their GISs do not match to their administrative environments.

Another problem is how to deal with the speed of technological innovation. IT related technologies develop too fast and revolutionarily for local governments to follow. Even during the time of constructing GIS in Korea, Information Technology has been continuously and rapidly developed. When a GIS construction project is finished, the system soon becomes outmoded and incompatible with newly developed techniques such as Mobile GIS and Internet GIS.

In many cases, it is more expensive to readjust the outmoded system than to construct a completely new one. It is not wise for a local government to try to keep an old system due to their concerns of sunk costs. Ironically, the first early investment can be a more serious obstacle in the development of a comprehensive system later. Investing strategy sometimes requires drastic changes.

Also other problems arise from incompatible software among departments and bureaus of local governments. The frequent and fundamental changes of hardware technology accompanying new software result in the problem of incompatibility among neighboring systems. Especially when local governments compete with each other to have the most advanced version of a system, this problem of difficulty in exchange of information arises.

Legal and Institutional Limitations

Major legal and institutional limitations originate from personnel systems such as frequent personnel mobility, promotion ceilings for technicians and other legal arrangements. In the personnel administration system used by Korean local governments, employees change their positions very often, and because rank system, they are supposed to be generalists rather than specialists by experiencing various administrative positions.

GIS professionals holding technical positions with some experience of GIS are continuously moving to other positions periodically searching for promotions. However, it takes a long time to construct a GIS in local governments. If GIS professionals change their positions in two or three years, it would be difficult for them to accumulate GIS technology or even follow up newly developing technologies.

Promotion ceilings for technicians work against the accumulation of GIS technology. There exist promotion ceilings for technical positions up to certain high-level positions in Korean governmental organizations. The hierarchical ladder of Korean civil service is designed so that the possibility of a promotion for technical personnel is closed to certain positions, which thus leads to those who want a higher rank transferring themselves to management jobs.

Naturally, GIS professionals holding technical positions want to transfer to general management positions in pursuit of promotions. Where general positions are preferred to technical positions, technicians can find no incentives to stick to the difficult and laborious job of constructing GIS in local governments. As a result, GIS professionals holding technical positions are continuously moving to other positions periodically and finally transfer to general management positions. Under this personnel system, it is difficult to accumulate GIS technology skills in local governments.

Organization Behavioral and Cultural Limitations

For successful GIS implementation, creativity and cooperation is indispensable. However, public officials are accustomed to the bureaucratic and authoritative organizational culture of Korea. Under the strong bureaucratic control of government organizations, they have conservative organizational behaviors, thereby somewhat resisting organizational reform influenced by the introduction of GIS.

Most of the Korean public employees are career seekers which results in the perpetuation of power politics inside bureaucracy. Civil servants hope to be appointed to the most powerful positions in their agencies and once they acquire these positions, they want to maintain the current organizational structures and cultures.

Not only general public officials but also GIS technicians resist to organizational changes. Because GIS technology changes organization structure, public officials and GIS professionals resist GIS related organizational changes.

Another problem is that the recognition of GIS among higher bureaucrats is especially low. Elected officials and political appointees think the GIS of local governments as less important when compared to street level bureaucrats. A recent survey of the city of Kyongsan revealed that 40 percent of local policy makers agreed to the introduction of GIS, while 57 percent of street level bureaucrats agreed.

Due to the discrepancy between the technical understanding of Internet GIS and the low acknowledgement of GIS among local government leadership, it is hard for local governments to keep strong incentives when implementing GIS.

Database Related Limitations

Databases are at the heart of GIS. If data is not correct, all information systems are useless. When it comes to databases, maintenance is the most important job of all. After the completion of digital mapping, its maintenance is required in order to make GIS a success. A better utilization of GIS indispensably requires attribute data. Usually, social statistical data are used as attribute data by local governments.

In Korea, the Korean Statistics Administration collects all data including local data for national purposes. Local governments do not have enough financial resources to produce and maintain their own local databases. This centralization of national data is an obstacle unless there were close linkages between the central and local governments.

Another problem is that legal districts such as administrative boundaries, postal areas, electoral districts and education districts are not identical. Before constructing databases, a prerequisite is to rearrange legal districts and boundaries for the efficient database construction of GIS (Kim, 1999).

Recommendations

In order to overcome the limitations of GIS applications for local governments, this study recommends alternative approaches such as cost efficient GIS, decentralized GIS, citizen oriented GIS and geographic e-government.

Cost-efficient and Effective GIS

In the construction of GIS, local governments could utilize cost efficient or effective approaches. Without the justification of cost efficiency, GIS projects cannot be supported in an era of financial austerity. For a successful cost-benefit analysis, the goal of GIS should be defined at the beginning of GIS construction and more careful attention should be paid to intangible benefits. According to a case study on cost-benefit analysis, Daegu Metropolitan GIS has payback periods of 24 years with the discount rate of 4 percent and 25 years with the discount rate of 6 percent (Kim, 2004).

A typological cost-benefit analysis shows that land information systems, transportation information systems and property tax systems are more cost-efficient than GISs with facility management (Kim at al., 2003). As mentioned above, Korean local governments show very low financial independence rates. Under this circumstance, Korean local governments need to adopt a cost-efficient GIS at first and then expand GIS into other areas such as facility management .

Decentralized GIS

In Korea, the central government maintained all the control over provincial and metropolitan and local governments before the decentralization reform. This situation still continues in a sense. Without the help of central government, local governments cannot implement their GISs. Because their financial independence rates are very low, the role classification of central and local governments is unclear. The success of GIS in local governments depends upon metropolitan and provincial governments as well as central government assistance.

The central government must play a coordinating and assisting role for local governments in pursuit of national interests. Relying on the mechanism of financial assistance, the central government must not try to control local governments because local governments are situated at the best place to judge their own needs of GIS. The present inter-governmental relations (IGR) of GIS should be re-arranged effectively due to the condition of decentralized GIS.

Citizen-oriented GIS

One of the key trends of constructing GIS in Korea is that local governments emphasized internal utilities and relatively ignored the GIS needs of their citizens. In the first stage of NGIS, this trend was not a problem. However, this can be a serious mistake at the second stage of NGIS. Local governments should work for internal efficiency as well as citizen satisfaction.

With the explosion of Internet business, citizens become more acquainted with information systems and develop their own demands. As the candle light demonstrations showed, the civil engagement in Korean public affairs is very vivid and strong. People actively express their needs and thoughts and exchange their ideas via the internet. Internet became the most powerful and rapid tool of communication in Korea.

Alongside e-Government, there are also many ways for citizens to participate in local affairs. People's mentalities are changing as they use the internet to the extent that they become impatient and more direct in expressing their demands. In accordance with citizens' demands of GIS and external utility, citizen oriented GIS is required. By making their citizens satisfied, local governments can justify their GIS projects such as Sungnam City's department of civil engineering did. This citizen-oriented GIS enables their citizens to easily access GIS by way of internet.

Note

This chapter was originally published in Kim, K. 2008. Geographic Information and Technology Administration in Korean Local Governments, *The Korean Journal of Local Government Studies* 12(3).

References

Busan Metropolitan City. 1997. *A Master Plan of Urban Information Management and Computerization Using GIS.*

Daegu Metropolitan City. 1999. *A Study on the Urban Information System.*

Ministry of Construction and Transportation. 2000. *A Report for a Hearing on the National GIS Master Plan of Korea (2001–2005).*

Seoul Development Institute. 1993. *A Study on the Construction of Seoul Metropolitan City GIS (I).*

_______. 1994. *A Study on the Construction of Seoul Metropolitan City GIS (II).*

Budic, Z.D. and D.R., Godschalk. 1996. Human Factors in Adoption of Geographic Information systems: A Local Government Case Study, *Public Administration Review* 56(6): 554–67.

Brown, M.M. and J.L., Brudney. 1998. A 'Smarter, Better, Faster, and Cheaper' Government Contracting and Geographic Information Systems, *Public Administration Review* 58(4): 335–45.

Campbell, H.J. 1993. GIS Implementation In British Local Government, In I., Masser and H.J., Onsrud. eds. *Diffusion and Use of Geographic Information Technologies*, London: Kluwer Academic Publishers.

Campbell, H. 1994. How Effective are GIS in Practice? A Case Study of British Local Government, *Information Systems* 8(3): 309–25.

Carr, T.R. 2003. Geographic Information Systems in the Public Sector, In G. David Garson. ed. *Public Information Technology: Policy and Management Issues,* 2003. London: Idea Group Publishing.

Garson, G.D. 2003. *Public Information Technology: Policy and Management Issues,* London: Idea Group Publishing.

Greene, R.W. 2001. *Open Access: GIS in e-Government,* Redlands, California: ESRI Press.

Harder, C. 1998. *Serving Maps on the Internet: Geographic Information on the World Wide Web,* Redlands, California: ESRI Press.

Greisler, D.S. and R.J., Stupak. 2007. *Handbook of Technology Management in Public Administration,* London: Taylor & Francis.

Heeks, R. ed. 1999. *Reinventing Government in the Information Age: International Practice in IT-enables Public Sector Reform,* London: Routledge.

Huxhold, W.E. and A.G., Levinsohn. 1995. *Managing Geographic Information System Projects,* New York: Oxford University Press.

Kim, K. 1998. Analysing GIS Implementation Factors in Local Governments, *Journal of the Korean Association of Geographic Information Studies* 1(2): 26–36.

_______. 1999. Construction and Application of GIS in Local Government: Theories and Practices. *Journal of Korean Association for Local Government Studies* 1(2): 149–69.

_______. 2004. Applying a Simulation Technique to Benefit Cost Analysis of GIS: A Case Study of Daegu City, Korea. *International Review of Public Administration* 9(1): 89–95.

_______, Fukui, H., Jo, M. and Lee, H. 2003. *Developing an Optimized Integration Model Based on Typological Benefit Cost Analysis of UIS in Korean and Japan* Taegu: Jungmoon.

Kraemer, K. and J., King. 1979. *A Requium for USAC,* The Regents of the University of California, Irvine, California.

Kramer, K. J., King., D., Dunkle, and J., Lane. 1989. *Managing Information Systems: Change and Control in Organizational Computing,* San Francisco: Jossey-Bass.

Leonard-Barton, D. 1987. Implementing Structured Software Methodologies: A Case of Innovation in Process Technology, *Interfaces* 17: 6–17.

Masser, I. 1998. *Governments and Geographic Information,* London: Taylor & Francis.

_______. and Campbell, H. 1993. The Impact of GIS on Local Government in Great Britain, In Paul M. Mather ed. *Geographical Information Handling: Research and Applications,* New York: John Wiley & Sons.

Nolan, R. 1979. Managing the Crisis in Data Processing, *Harvard Business Review* March–April.

Obermeyer, N.J. and J.K., Pinto. 1994. *Managing Geographic Information Systems,* New York: The Quilford Press.

O'Looney, J. 2000. *Beyond Maps: GIS and Decision Making in Local Government,* New York: ESRI Press.

Onsrud, H.J. and J.K., Pinto. 1991. Diffusion of Geographic Information Innovations, *International Journal of Geographical Information Systems* 5(4): 447–67.

Pinto, J.K. and H.J., Onsrud. 1991. Correlating Adoption Factors and Adoption Characteristics with Successful Use of Geographic Information Systems, In M., Ian and H.J., Onsrud. eds. *Diffusion and Use of Geographic Information Technologies* London: Klurwer Academic Publishers.

Snellen, I., Th., M. and van de Donk, W.B.H.J. 1998. *Public Administration in an Information Age* Amsterdam: IOS Press.

Ventura, S.J. 1995. The Use of Geographical Information Systems in Local Government, *Public Administration Review* 55(5): 461–67.

Part V

Conclusion

Chapter 11 |

Conclusion

TOBIN IM AND GREG PORUMBESCU

In chapter four of his book *Time and Public Policy* entitled "Political Man vs. Economic Man" T. Alexander Smith discusses the differences between individuals who are politically motivated versus those who are economically motivated. In his discussion he introduces the idea of time preference and explains how economic man incorporates much more of a long-term perspective when making his decisions in an effort to stabilize his accumulation of wealth over time. Economic man's low time preference results from his desire to protect and increase the value of his assets and resources over time for the reason that he in fact owns resources. In contrast, the political man is not the owner of resources but rather a 'manager' of them (Smith, 1989), and must work to meet the immediate demands of citizens in order to maintain his position in the future. Consequently political man places a preference upon meeting the short term needs of the people he serves in hopes of obtaining long term job stability for himself. Thus society begins to look to the government more often than not to remedy problems which have historically been considered private. Smith more succinctly explains this phenomena by stating that the "growing politicization of problems traditionally thought to be non-political can only shorten time horizons."(1989, 24) Thus in the name of sustainability it is obvious that long term horizons are necessary, and economic man is best suited to pursue sustainable policies than political man. Hence when a government introduces a fundamental reform, such as decentralization, to its political system, proper timing in light of its economic history is necessary.

Time as a Critical Factor

It is a safe assumption that the citizens of poor countries would choose a wealthy life over enhanced political participation if they could choose just one. Based on the discussion made by T. Alexander Smith it is possible to infer that, for developing nations, the idea of increased democratization possesses the potential to overpoliticize issues and thereby jeopardize long term development. Thus, in the name of development, it may be wise to reconsider immediate democratization reforms. In this vein we must also consider utility of market led economic development, which as Alice M. Rivlin puts it, are "essentially an extreme form of decentralization" in that market models move "the locus of decisions about how services should be produced not simply to the community, but to the individual consumer". Consequently, under such conditions, a united national direction in terms of development is kept to a minimum and a great deal of pressure is placed upon administrative infrastructure which may not yet be capable of operating in such conditions.

The conclusion we can draw from the above is that while political development, or democratization, is of course an important aspect of all nations' development, it is not something which should be rushed. By decreasing the role of the government too early a nation risks straining its administrative capabilities and developing without a direction which is in fact tantamount to not developing at all. Thus the role of the central government with regards to development must not be understated.

The best example to support this assertion is the United States. Newly independent and extremely wary of central governments the founding fathers of the United States initially elected to structure their government as a confederacy of states. Thus the central government was granted minimal power and essentially had no authority over the states. As time progressed many of the states, which were all very different from one another in terms of wealth, size and available resources, pursued different paths of development; thus there was one nation moving in 13 different directions. The results of this arrangement came to a head during Shay's Rebellion, when the federal government was incapable of putting down a minor rebellion due to the fact that it had no authority to raise funds, tax the states and lacked the ability to raise an army. Eventually the rebellion was quelled and the founding fathers of the United States decided to increase the role and power of the central government by switching to a federal system which remains to this day.

Economic Development in South Korea: A Case of Avoiding Political Pitfalls?

South Korea's rapid rise to prominence on the global stage, in fact occurred at two different paces; political and economic. Following the end of a very devastating civil war, South Korea was not only in ruins but also represented the more rural half of a now divided peninsula. The population was extremely poor and highly susceptible to starvation, the infrastructure entirely erased and long-term prospects for a successful Korea were nearly entirely overshadowed by a need to ease current deficits and shortages. It is within this context that we might begin to understand why economic development and reforms were pursued to a much greater than democratizing reforms. At the helm of this new nation was a central government which was quickly centralizing political tasks and consolidating its power in order to make it the sole source of dominance within the nation.

Consequently, during much of the second half of the 20th century in Korea all roads led to Seoul. Despite provisions having been made with varying degrees of sincerity, regarding local autonomy, the truth of the matter was that the central government did not intend to loosen its tight grip on the affairs of the nation. The central government set the agenda, implemented it and enforced it with an iron fist, giving Korean citizens little if any opportunity to influence the president's agenda. To many modern political scientists such behavior constitutes a violation of citizen's rights and consequently leaders of this era are often portrayed as morally compromised individuals whose primary focus was to ensure their own perpetual political influence. Perhaps such portrayals of these individuals is valid, however one must ask the question of whether the long-term results of their policies and uncompromising regimes were indicative of tyranny or of a single-minded dedication to the country's rapid development.

In order to portray regimes which resist implementing decentralization or democratic reforms as tyrannical, democracy must be deemed to be a panacea, a cure for everything that ails a country and something that must be immediately implemented in order to advance the development of a nation. Under such theories we can surmise that leaders who avoid implementing democracy are more concerned with maintaining their own influential roles in government, than they are with improving the wellbeing of their population. However we know that democracy is actually not a panacea and despite being a good principle in general, there are numerous cases which prove that in fact, democracy is not the solution to all the problems confronting a nation. Consequently a key, if not main task of modern governments, is identifying what areas to extend democracy, as well as which areas to reduce democracy and when.

Why is Decentralization so Difficult?

As previously mentioned, in the context of this book democratization is synonymous with decentralization. In developing or newly founded nations, the importance of decentralization reforms is generally viewed as paramount however paradoxically these types of reforms are also extremely risky because often times these nations lack sufficient infrastructure to implement decentralization reforms in their entirety, and consequently are actually harmed by the attempted increase of decentralization (Davoodi and Zoo, 1998). Thus for developing nations which lack mature government institutions and stability, the question of extending democracy or decentralization is complicated and problematic. In light of this we can infer that decentralizing reforms which worked well in developed nations are by no means guaranteed to work in developing or less developed nations—contextual considerations must be made if reforms are to be successful.

For developing nations economic development is in most cases considered a means to an end, and consequently the role of the markets waxes and the role of the government wanes. Along these lines governments, as well as scholars, often times place greater emphasis upon the market's role in economic development and deemphasize the role of government. Such beliefs are best showcased by countless privatization and decentralization reforms which have been pursued by many governments throughout the world in an attempt to increase the level of governmental efficiency, enhance citizen participation and boost economic development (Martinez and McNab, 2003). However, the pursuit of such objectives should not be forced; economic development necessitates the cultivation of a stable government due to the fact that it is the government which creates the environment in which markets function. Thus, notions of government and economic development are not divorced and instead should be considered complimentary.

The events experienced in Korea related to its development and advancement provide an interesting example of a staggered approach to development. Perhaps it is this staggered approach which enabled the government at the time to avoid many of the developmental pitfalls other developing nations experience along their path to advancement. Rather than immediately seeking to delegate power and responsibility to several smaller units, the Korean Government pursued a unified approach and in doing so did not deny the importance of the government's role in economic development. This approach resulted in granting the central government a great degree of power which allowed the government to function more concertedly and assert itself as a driving force in the advancement of Korea.

Strengths of Korean Decentralization

The concept of development is generally acknowledged as having two core components; economic and political. Commonly decentralization is seen as a means of achieving both aspects simultaneously and thus decentralization reforms are implemented with expectations that, by moving decision making and the provision of goods to lower levels of government, efficiency gains will be made, democracy enhanced and costs cut (Grindle, 2007). However in the process of deciding such an issue it appears that the leaders seeking to implement such reforms are focusing too much on the general picture and not giving enough thought to why such reforms may not yet be appropriate; in other words there is not thought about contextual considerations when implementing such reforms.

This book has sought to discuss some of the issues related to the task of decentralization and development in the context of South Korea and assessed the impact of decentralization reforms on three general categories; economic development, citizen participation and administrative efficiency. The effects of decentralization on their respective category were then explained more in depth by the articles included in that section.

What has been made apparent by now is that in the context of South Korea, decentralization reforms are in fact not always beneficial. In part two of this book which dealt with economic development, the point was made that by initiating such reforms too early, governments risk rendering their political systems inefficient by distracting them with numerous side issues. Consequently these issues detract from the government's administrative capacity and decrease the government's ability to effectively deal with more critical issues of development.

However, once decentralization reforms have been implemented and the role of sub-national governments is increased, local and regional governments tend to exhibit the following tendencies: increasing social policies, or continuing development policies, pursuing both or pursuing neither. The path taken in most cases is dependent upon several socio-economic and political factors such as; mayors' educational background, fiscal capacity and the degree of support local politicians receive from their constituents. At this point it is apparent that a national direction in terms of development is lost and replaced by more individualized or specific paths. Consequently the argument can be made that if decentralization reforms are implemented too early, regional disparity can also be enhanced.

One possible method of development available to regional governments and often times seen as having great potential for poorer regions is the introduction of casinos in hopes that their well-known attributes of being highly profitable and popular will prevail and help revitalize the growth of an area. However such beliefs tend to be misguided in fact because as chapter 5 has demonstrated, the effects of casinos on growth are actually not that far reaching. While providing the government with increased tax revenues and bringing more jobs to the region, the impact of a casino in fact is not really felt by those who are not directly involved in its operations.

In part III which deals with citizen participation, the first chapter examines the impact of cyber participation on local governments. By initiating cyber participation methods it has been demonstrated that local governments are in fact better able to realize the intent of decentralization reforms in that local government's efficiency and participation is increased. The reason why cyber participation is so beneficial is because it provides citizens with increased and more diverse points of access to the local government, most of which are free from time constraints. Thus citizens have more opportunities for genuine participation and opinion expression.

In the case of more traditional methods of citizen participation in local governance, findings are much more mixed in that they demonstrate a much less genuine degree of participation. Despite citizens displaying an eagerness to take part in the local decision making process, local governments demonstrated a tendency to make selective use of citizen's opinions. In addition the methods available to citizens to express their opinions were also limited thereby further restricting citizen participation. Therefore, increases in citizen participation are largely based upon government support; even if decentralization reforms are implemented, meaningful increases in citizen participation cannot be assumed to follow.

In addition to increased participation and improved economic development, decentralization reforms are also purported to improve administrative efficiency. The reality of such claims as experienced in Korea, were assessed in the fourth section of this book. The first case examine the reality of claimed efficiency gains which accompany decentralization reforms focused on the proliferation of quagos in South Korea during the mid to late 1990s. Following the example of western nations, Korean local and regional governments pursued a 'quagocratization' of many services which ultimately resulted in creating a large grey area of administrative oversight in that there was no clear body which was charged with holding quagos accountable for their performance, consequently they were given much more leeway in terms of performance standards. Additionally a great amount of overlap was exhibited in that frequently regional and local governments would both establish quagos charged with performing the same task, thereby resulting in the inefficient distribution of services.

The following chapter of this book reassesses service distribution along the lines of central provision versus more localized provision, namely at the regional and municipal levels. The findings here demonstrate that economies of scale help to make the central government more efficient in the provision of services; however the problem of corruption also tends to be more pronounced under centralized methods of provision. Therefore perhaps the most appropriate level for the distribution of services, which would take advantage of economies of scale while reducing corruption, would be the regional level.

The final chapter dealt with implementing new technology in order to enhance organizational efficiency. The specific example which was assessed here was the use of Geographic Information Systems (GIS) in assisting central and local governments. Due to substantial initial outlays of capital, as well as administrative, technical and socio-economic limitations, the implementation of GISs is difficult for local governments. However, in spite of the difficulties associated with implementing such a system, it must be pursued due to the great efficiency gains GIS offers which will ultimately help local governments better perform the tasks they are increasingly being charged with performing. Thus in order to avoid some of the difficulties associated with implementing GIS, the author suggests three implementation methods local governments could employ; cost efficient and effective GIS, Decentralized GIS and citizen oriented GIS.

References

Davoodi, H and H.F., Zou. 1998. Fiscal Decentralization and Economic Growth: A Cross-Country Study, *Journal of Urban Economics* 43: 244–57.

Grindle, M.S. 2007. Going Local: Decentralization, Democratization, and the Promise of Good Governance, Princeton, NJ: Princeton University Press.

Moskowitz, K. 1982. Korean Development and Korean Studies—A Review Article, *Journal of Asian Studies* 42: 1.

Park, N.W. 2010. Political Decentralization and Fiscal Management of Local Governments: Evidence and Lessons from Korea, Center for Fiscal Analysis, Korea Institute of Public Finance. Seoul, South Korea. (Accessed January 8th)

Rivlin, A.M. 1971. Systemic Thinking for Social Action, Washington, D.C.: The Brookings Institution.

Smith, T.A. 1989. Time and Public Policy, Knoxville, TN: University of Tennessee Press.